Petr Spodniak

Mikael Collan

Satu Viljainen

EXAMINING THE MARKETS FOR NORDIC ELECTRICITY PRICE AREA DIFFERENTIALS (EPAD) - FOCUS ON FINLAND

20.5.2015

LUT Scientific and Expertise Publications
Raportit ja selvitykset – Reports, No. 51

ISBN 978-952-265-775-6
ISBN 978-952-265-776-3 (PDF)
ISSN 2243-3384
Lappeenranta University of Technology
2015

Executive Summary

The Nordic electricity market is often identified as one of the best functioning super-national electricity markets in the World, this widely spread understanding is often extended to cover all aspects of the Nordic electricity market. The Nordic electricity market maintains a system spot price for electricity and on the connected financial markets electricity future contracts exist to allow hedging the system price risk. As the Nordic electricity markets are segmented into multiple price areas, whose electricity price may differ from the spot price, Electricity Price Area Differentials (EPAD) are available for hedging the risk caused by the area price difference. In other words, to completely hedge a position in the Nordic electricity markets a market participant must obtain a hedge against the system price risk and the risk caused by the possible area price – system price difference.

In order for the Nordic electricity markets to function well it is important that market participants have a possibility to fully hedge themselves against the price risk. In fact, many market participants, such as public organizations may have in place policies that do not allow them to keep un-hedged market positions on electricity. In this vein and in the absence of recent research on the markets for hedging electricity prices in the Nordic electricity markets, this report studies the markets of the Electricity Price Area Differentials (EPAD) in general and specifically the EPAD markets of the Price Area covering Finland (HEL/FI).

The goal of this report is to present descriptive data on EPAD trading and to describe the market conditions that exist for trading EPAD contracts. Some preliminary conclusions about the functionality of the markets for EPAD contracts are drawn.

Keywords: Nordic electricity markets, electricity price area differentials, EPAD, risk management

Yhteenveto

Pohjoismaista sähkömarkkinaa pidetään usein yhtenä parhaiten toimivista ylikansallisista sähkömarkkinoista maailmassa, tämä laajalle levinnyt käsitys ulotetaan usein käsittämään kaikki pohjoismaisen sähkömarkkinaan littyvät toiminnot. Pohjoismaisilla sähkömarkkinoilla ylläpidetään sähkön systeemi spot hintaa ja sähkömarkkinoihin liittyvillä rahoitusmarkkinoilla käydään kauppaa sähköfutuureilla joilla voidaan suojautua hintavaihteluilta. Pohjoismaiset sähkömarkkinat ovat jakautuneet hinta-alueesiin, joiden sähkön hinta voi erota systeemi spot hinnasta. Näiden hintaerojen luomilta riskeiltä suojautumiseksi on luotu ns. sähkön aluehintaerosopimukset (eng. Electricity Price Area Differentials, EPAD). Toisin sanoen, suojautuakseen kokonaan sähkön hintariskeiltä tulee pohjoismaisilla sähkömarkkinoilla toimivan toimijan suojautua sekä systeemihinnan, että aluehintaerojen aiheuttamilta riskeiltä.

Jotta pohjoismaiset sähkömarkkinat toimisivat hyvin on tärkeää, että markkinaosapuolilla on mahdollisuus tarvittaessa suojata itsensä täysin sähkön hintariskiltä. Itse asiassa, tiettyjen markkinoilta sähköä ostavien tahojen, kuten julkisten toimijoiden voimassa oleva suojauspolitiikka saattaa edellyttää niiden suojaavan sähkön hintapositionsa kokonaan. Tähän liittyen ja tuoreen tutkimustiedon lähes kokonaan puuttuessa tämä raportti tutkii sähkön aluehintasopimusten (EPAD) markkinoita yleisesti ja erityisesti Suomen alueelle (HEL/FI) kohdistuvien aluehintasopimusten markkinoita.

Raportin tarkoitus on esitellä kuvailevaa tietoa aluehintasopimusten kaupankäynnistä ja kuvailla näiden sopimusten kaupankäynnille olemassa olevaa markkinatilannetta. Lisäksi esitetään joitakin alustavia johtopäätöksiä koskien aluehintasopimusten markkinoitten toimivuutta.

Avainsanat: Pohjoismainen sähkömarkkina, sähkön aluehintasopimukset, EPAD, riskien hallinta

Summary of main findings

The main findings of this report are listed here shortly for easy access. The main findings are listed in the order in which they can be found from the report.

The average daily closing prices of EPAD contracts of all maturities for Helsinki and Stockholm changed notably from year to year. The average daily closing price for yearly contracts for Helsinki was above the average daily closing price for Stockholm (Swedish price area 3) for the whole studied period 2007-2014.

For Helsinki and Stockholm the average actual trade prices were different for trades traded through the electronic trading system (ETS, exchange) and trades over the counter (OTC). The size of the difference varied from year to year.

The average daily closing price (Daily Fix) was notably different from the average actual trade prices for Helsinki for all contract maturities. The average daily closing price has been lower than the average actual trade prices every year for yearly contracts since 2008.

The daily closing price (Daily Fix) did not include the information contained in any over the counter (OTC) trades.

Volatility of closing prices for EPADs for Helsinki and Stockholm changed dramatically from year to year and the volatilities of closing prices for contracts with all maturities were over 20% for all studied years.

The average absolute spread (in EUR) for Helsinki was higher than for Stockholm for all studied years for all contract maturities. The average spread as a percentage of the best ask price has changed from year to year for all contract maturities. The average spread as a percentage of the best ask price was above 10% for all studied years and for all contract maturities.

Daily spread in EUR and as % of the best ask bid varied notably during the trading period for the studied contracts.

For EPAD markets in general, more trades took place OTC than through the ETS system for every studied year. OTC accounted for ~75% of all contracts traded in the Nordic EPAD markets.

For Helsinki and Stockholm the average number of contracts traded per trade was higher for OTC trades than for trades through the ETS for all contract maturities for all studied years. OTC accounted for around eighty percent of the overall volume of EPADs traded.

Measured by traded volume Helsinki and Stockholm (Sweden) were the most important price areas. More than 85% of Helsinki total volume was traded OTC for all studied years.

For the majority of trading days during studied (case) EPAD contract's trading time there were no actual trades recorded (OTC or through the ETS). The daily spread changed dramatically during the trading period of the studied (case) EPAD contract's trading time.

Tärkeimmät löydökset (FIN)

Raportin tärkeimmät löydökset on listattu tähän helposti saataville. Löydökset on listattu samassa järjestyksessä, missä ne löytyvät raportin tekstistä.

Päivittäisen EPAD sopimusten päätöshinnan keskiarvo vaihteli huomattavasti vuodesta toiseen kaiken pituisille sopimuksille (kuukausi, vuosineljännes, vuosi) Helsingin ja Tukholman hinta-alueilla. Keskimääräinen päivittäinen päätöshinta alueella Helsinki oli korkeampi kuin alueella Tukholma (Ruotsi 3) kaikkina tarkasteltuina vuosina 2007-2014.

Hinta-alueille Helsinki ja Tukholma keskimääräinen elektronisen kaupankäyntijärjestelmän (ETS) kautta tehtyjen kauppojen hinta erosi over the counter tehtyjen kauppojen keskimäärisestä hinnasta. Keskimääräinen hintaero vaihteli vuodesta toiseen.

Keskimääräinen päivittäinen päätöshinta (Daily Fix) erosi huomattavasti keskimääräisestä tehtyjen kauppojen hinnasta hinta-alueen Helsinki kaiken pituisille sopimuksille. Kekimääräinen päivittäinen päätöshinta on ollut alempi kuin keskimääräinen tehtyjen kauppojen hinta jokaiselle vuodelle, vuodesta 2008 lähtien.

Päivittäiseen päätöshintaan (Daily Fix) ei ole sisältynyt over the counter (OTC) tehtyjen kauppojen sisältämää informaatiota.

Päätöshintojen volatiliteetti hinta-alueilla Helsinki ja Tukholma vaihteli dramaattisesti vuodesta toiseen ja kaikken pituisten sopimusten volatiliteetti oli yli 20% tutkituille vuosille.

Keskimääräinen euromääräinen spread hinta-alueelle Helsinki oli suurempi kuin hinta-alueelle Tukholma kaikille tarkastelluille vuosille ja kaiken pituisille sopimuksille. Kaiken pituisten sopimusten keskimääräinen best bid hinnasta laskettu prosenttimääräinen spread vaihteli vuodesta toiseen ja pysytteli yli 10%:ssa kaikkina tarkasteltuina vuosina ja kaiken pituisille sopimuksille.

Päivittäinen euromääräinen ja prosenttina best bid hinnasta laskettu spread vaihtelihuomattavasti tutkittujen sopimusten vaihdanta-aikana.

Tehtyjen kauppojen lukumäärä oli suurempi OTC:n osalta kuin ETS:n kautta jokaisen tarkastellun vuoden osalta EPAD markkinalle kokonaisuutena. OTC kaupankäynnin osuus oli ~75% kaikista vaihdetuista sopimuksista Pohjoismaisessa EPAD markkinassa.

Helsingin ja Tukholman osalta OTC:n kautta vaihdettiin keskimäärin useampia sopimuksia per tehty kauppa kuin ETS:n kautta tehdyissä kaupoissa. Noin 80% vaihdetusta EPAD sopimusten kokonaisvolyymista vaihdettiin OTC kaupankäynnin kautta.

Vaihdetun volyymin perusteella Helsinki ja Tukholma (Ruotsi) olivat tärkeimmät hinta-alueet. Yli 85% Helsingin kokonaisvolyymista kaikille vuosille vaihdettiin OTC:n kautta.

Tarkasteltujen (case) sopimusten osalta suurinpana osana vaihdanta-ajan päivistä ei käyty lainkaan kauppaa (OTC tai ETS:n kautta). Tarkasteltujen (case) sopimusten päivittäinen spread vaihteli dramaattisesti vaihdanta-ajan aikana.

Table of contents

PART I – Introduction

PART II – Examination of EPAD markets

PART III – Illustrative cases

PART IV – Preliminary conclusions

PART V – Appendix

PART I

Introduction

1 Introduction

The Nordic power market is commonly used as an example of a successful multinational integrated electricity market. Initially, when formed in the 1990s, the Nordic power market was an alliance of the restructured electricity markets in Norway, Sweden, Finland, and Denmark. The primary target was more efficient sharing of resources (e.g., hydro power). In addition, the Nordic electricity market integration was aligned with the world-wide restructuring wave of the 1990s. Today, also the Baltic countries have become a part of the Nordic power market, after joining the common Nordic market place for electricity, Nord Pool Spot.

In short, Nord Pool Spot organizes the market place for wholesale electricity trade that leads to physical delivery of electricity. Most importantly, Nord Pool Spot hosts the day-ahead Elspot market, where day-head electricity prices are formed for all hours of the following day (in addition, Nord Pool Spot is also a market place for intraday trading of electricity). The calculation of the day-ahead electricity spot prices in the Elspot market proceeds as follows. Every day by noon, Elspot buyers and sellers submit hour-by-hour bids (single hour, flexible hour, or block bids) to trade power for delivery the next day. All purchase and sell bids are then aggregated into hourly supply and demand curves, defining hourly prices and quantities for the following day. The hourly system price for each hour is obtained assuming an unconstrained flow in the Nordic power system. If this assumption also holds in reality, all Elspot orders are settled at the system price, regardless of the location of production and consumption.

In practice, however, network congestions often occur. In such cases, the market is split into pre-defined bidding areas, for which separate area prices are calculated. The area prices thus reflect both the infrastructure constraints, as well as the underlying production and consumption structures in each area. Whenever the market is split, the Elspot orders in different areas are settled at corresponding area prices. At present, there are 15 bidding areas in the Nordic market for which area prices are calculated, in case of network congestions.

To sum up, two sets of prices are calculated in the Nordic power market: one assuming no transmission constraints in the entire grid (system price), and one reflecting transmission bottlenecks between bidding areas (area prices). Both types of prices are tied to different types of risks, which can be hedged at the financial derivatives market operating in parallel with the spot market. A centralized marketplace for financial electricity derivative contracts that is, an Electronic Trading System (ETS), is organized by Nasdaq OMX Commodities. In addition, financial contracts can also be traded over the counter (OTC) and bilaterally.

In the Nordic power market, the derivatives that are traded in the exchange include base and peak load futures, deferred settlement futures (DS Futures), options, and Electricity Price Area Differentials (EPAD). Stemming from the day-ahead market logic outlined above, the Nordic power derivatives can be generally divided into two categories: the futures contracts that hedge the system price risk and the EPAD contracts that hedge the area price risk. To put it in a different way: for futures contracts, the underlying reference price is the Nordic system price, and for the EPAD contracts, it is the difference between the area price and the Nordic system price.

With respect to the EPAD contracts in particular, the question about the liquidity of the markets has occasionally been raised. In 2010, for example, the Nordic energy regulators voiced their concern about the liquidity in contracts for difference (CfD, now EPAD) (NordReg, 2010). Since then, no public evaluation of the EPAD market has been conducted. However, being an essential risk management instrument in the Nordic power market, the liquidity of EPAD contracts is of importance. Moreover, the issue has become more relevant as area prices have started to occur more often.

In this report, we focus on the EPAD markets in general and the EPADs traded for the price area Finland (Helsinki) in particular. For comparison, the data from the price area Sweden 3 (Stockholm) is on several occasions also looked at in detail. To shed light on the current state of the EPAD markets, we elaborate on issues such as:

- the development and volatility of the daily closing prices of EPAD contracts of different maturities;

- the volumes of EPAD contracts traded through the electronic trading system and over the counter;

- the mechanism used to determine the EPAD contract closing price absent actual trades through the electronic trading system;

- the development of daily spreads of EPAD contracts of different maturities.

The report is constructed as follows. Chapter 2 gives a short presentation of the data used. Chapter 3 concentrates on the EPAD price development and price volatility. Chapter 4 discusses EPAD spreads. Chapter 5 looks at the EPAD market activity. Chapters 6 through 8 discuss specific EPAD contracts as cases. Finally, Chapter 9 summarizes some conclusions and presents future research directions.

2. Data

The data set used in this report was acquired from and provided by NASDAQ OMX Commodities, the "exchange" for trading the Nordic EPAD contracts.

The data used includes aggregated daily market data and intra-day-data for individual trades for the period January 3, 2005 – March 25, 2014.

Included are the trades made through the NASDAQ electronic trading system (ETS) and the over the counter (OTC) trades recorded in the system. Any bilateral trades made between parties are not included in the data.

Geographically, the data covers all price areas of the Nordic electricity market that have been active during the studied period.

Some specific issues about the price areas:

When in the analyses we refer to the price area "Stockholm" (STO) prior to November 2011, we actually refer to price area "Sweden". This is, because until November 2011 Sweden was a single price area. From November 2011 onwards, the "Sweden" price area was demerged into four separate price areas: Luleå (LUL/SE1), Sundsvall (SUN/SE2), Stockholm (STO/SE3), and Malmö (MAL/SE4).

PART II

Examination of EPAD markets

3. EPAD contract price

In this section we study the historical price levels of EPAD contracts. We study averages to gain an overall view of the price levels and we look at what kind of price changes happen during a single contract trading time. Focus is also put on how the daily closing price (Daily Fix) is determined by the exchange (NASDAQ OMX). We also take a short look at the volatility of EPAD contract prices:

First, we look at the average closing price level of EPAD contracts for each contract maturity (monthly, quarterly, and yearly) for contracts with delivery on different years for selected price areas.

Second, we look at the average actual trade price levels of EPAD contracts for each contract maturity (monthly, quarterly, and yearly) for contracts with delivery on different years for selected price areas for trades through the ETS and OTC separately.

Third, we look at the difference between the average closing price levels of EPAD contracts and the average actual trade price levels for trades conducted through the ETS and OTC for each contract maturity (monthly, quarterly, and yearly) for contracts with delivery on different years for Helsinki.

Fourth, we look at how, according to the NASDAQ OMX, the closing price (Daily Fix) for EPAD contracts is determined.

Fifth, we look at the development of the daily closing price (Daily Fix) and the actually executed trades of selected single EPAD contract for price area Helsinki in detail.

Sixth, we shortly look at the volatility of EPAD contract prices.

3.1. Average closing price level of EPAD contracts

We look at the average daily closing price (Daily Fix) levels of EPAD contracts of different maturities (monthly, quarterly, and yearly) for contracts with delivery on years 2007 – Q1 / 2014 for Helsinki (HEL) and Stockholm (STO) price areas. Price area Stockholm included the whole of Sweden until 2011, after 2011 we include the data for only the Stockholm price area (Swedish price area 3).

Figure 3.1. shows the average closing prices for monthly EPAD contracts for Helsinki and Stockholm for years 2007 – Q1/2014. One can see that the average closing prices seem to follow each other closely until the contracts for the year 2012, when the averages "separate". This coincides with the separation of the Sweden price area into four price areas. After 2012 the average closing price for EPADs for Helsinki was above the average closing price for Stockholm.

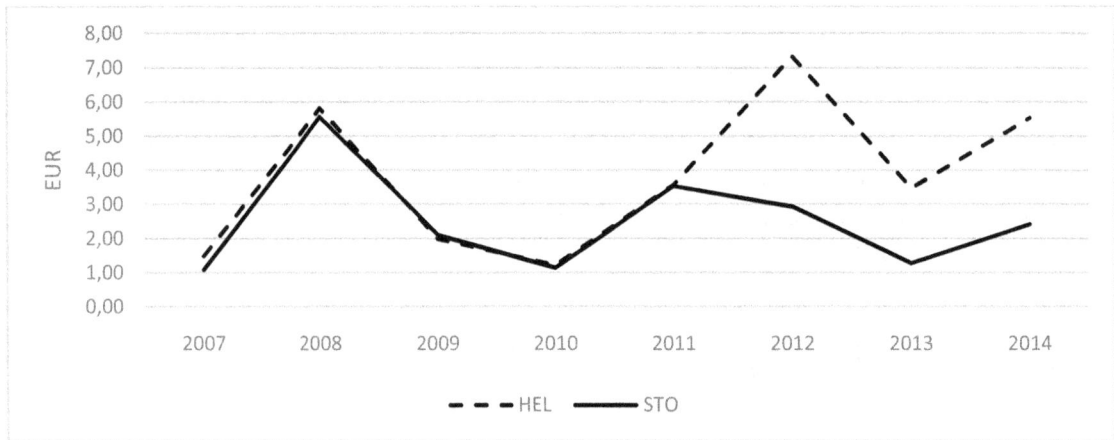

Figure 3.1. Average daily closing price in EUR for monthly EPAD contracts for Helsinki (HEL) and Stockholm (STO) for 2007 – 2014 (for 2014 the data is not complete)

Figure 3.2. shows the average daily closing price for quarterly EPAD contracts for Helsinki and Stockholm for years 2007 – Q1/2014. One can see that also for quarterly contracts the average closing prices for Helsinki and Stockholm seems to follow each other until the contracts for the year 2012. The average closing price for Helsinki was above the average closing price for Stockholm for all studied years.

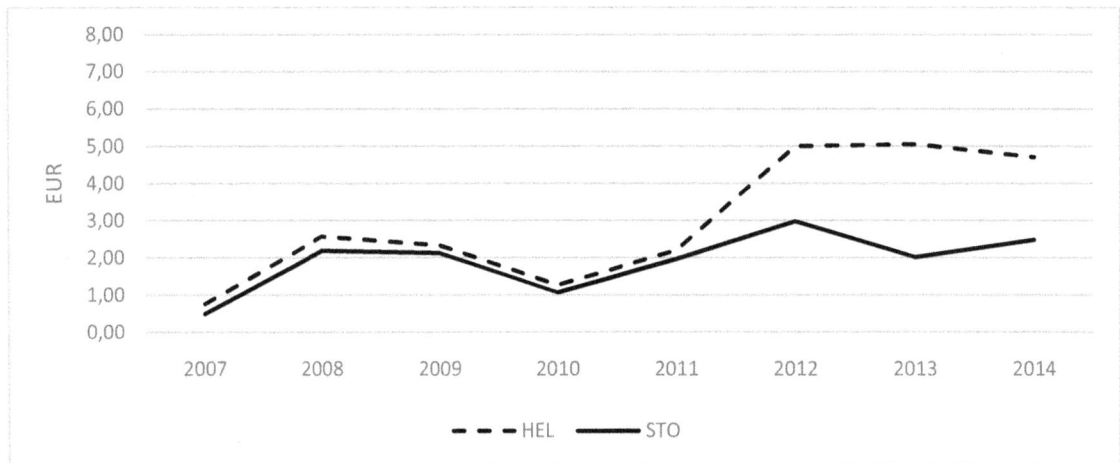

Figure 3.2. Average daily closing price in EUR for quarterly EPAD contracts for Helsinki (HEL) and Stockholm (STO) for 2007 – 2014 (for 2014 the data is not complete)

> **The average closing price of the monthly and the quarterly contracts for Helsinki and Stockholm "separate" for contracts for years after 2011.**

Figure 3.3. Show the average daily closing prices for yearly EPAD contracts for Helsinki and Stockholm for years 2007 – 2014. The average daily closing price for Helsinki was above the average closing price for Stockholm for all studied years. The absolute difference in the average daily closing prices for Helsinki and Stockholm in EUR was the lowest for 2007 contracts (about 0,29 EUR) and highest for 2014 contracts (about 1,46 EUR). The difference in the yearly contracts´ average daily closing price as a percentage of the STO average daily closing price between Helsinki and Stockholm was lowest for contracts for the year 2012 (about 33% of the STO average daily closing price) and the highest for the year 2008 (about 92% of the STO average daily closing price).

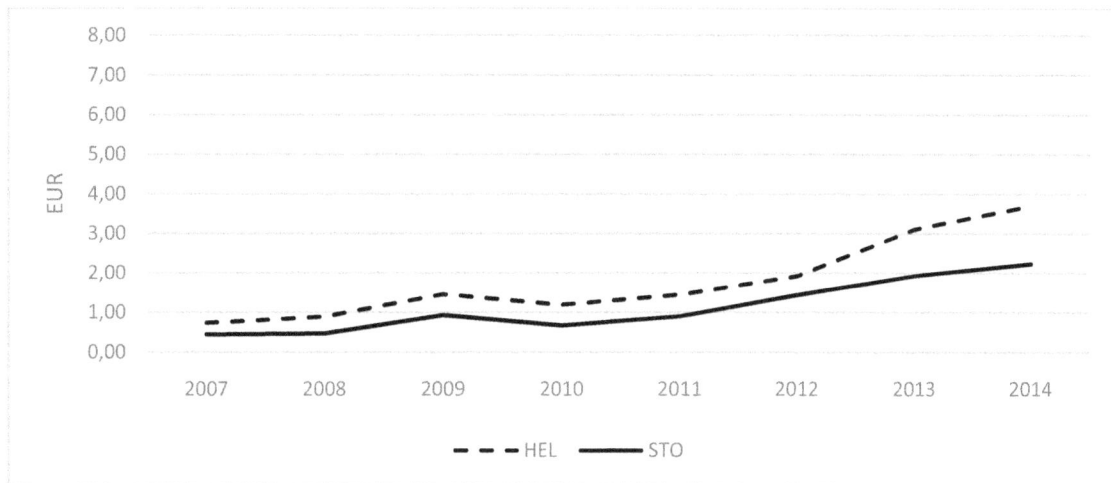

Figure 3.3. Average daily closing price in EUR for yearly EPAD contracts for Helsinki (HEL) and Stockholm (STO) for 2007 – 2014

> **The average daily closing price for yearly contracts for Helsinki was above the average daily closing price for Stockholm for all studied years.**

3.2. Average price levels of actual trades on EPAD contracts

We look at average actual trade price levels of EPAD contracts of different maturities (monthly, quarterly, and yearly) for contracts with delivery on years 2007 – Q1 / 2014 for Helsinki (HEL) and Stockholm (STO) price areas. Price area Stockholm included the whole of Sweden until 2011, after 2011 we include the data for only the Stockholm price area (Swedish price area 3). We look at the average trade prices of actual trades made through the ETS and OTC separately.

Figure 3.4. shows the average actual trade prices for monthly EPAD contracts for Helsinki and Stockholm for years 2007 – Q1/2014 separately for trades made through the ETS and OTC. One can see that the average actual trade prices seem to follow each other closely until the contracts for the year 2012, when the averages "separate". This coincides with the separation of the Sweden price area into four price areas. After 2012 the average actual trade price for EPADs for Helsinki was above the average actual trade prices for Stockholm for both the trades made through the ETS and OTC. The average actual trade price of trades made through the ETS differs from the average actual trade price OTC for both Helsinki and Stockholm. For Helsinki the smallest difference between the average OTC and the ETS traded actual prices is found for 2012 (about 0,26 EUR), for 2014 the difference was about 0,20 EUR, but the data is incomplete, the largest difference is found for 2008 (about 1,58 EUR).

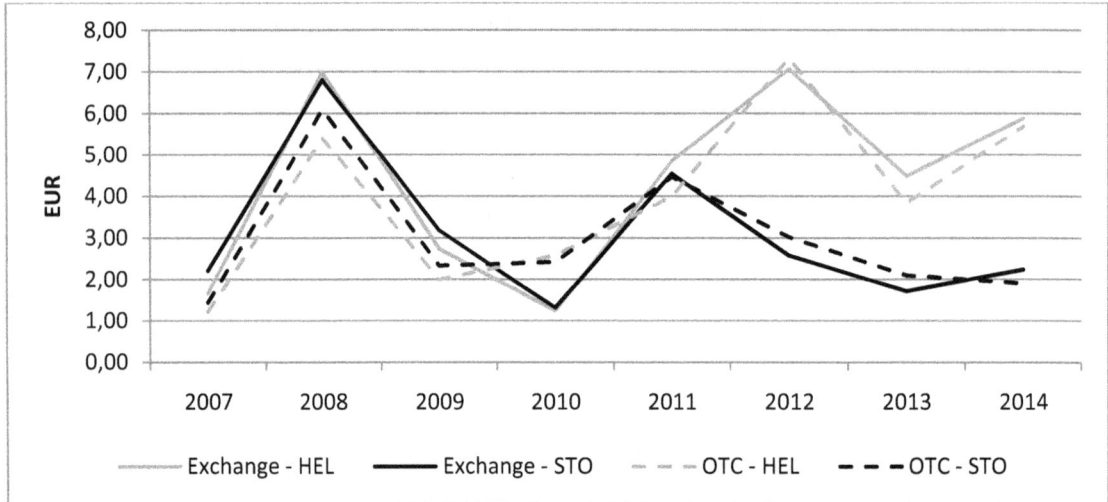

Figure 3.4. Average actual trade price in EUR for monthly EPAD contracts for Helsinki (HEL) and Stockholm (STO) 2007 – Q1/2014 (for 2014 the data is not complete), separately for trades through the ETS and OTC.

> **The average actual trade price for trades traded through the ETS differs from the trades traded OTC. The difference varies year to year.**

Figure 3.5. shows the average actual trade prices for quarterly EPAD contracts for Helsinki and Stockholm for years 2007 – Q1/2014 separately for trades made through the ETS and OTC. One can see that the average actual trade prices for the quarterly contracts seem to follow each other closely until the contracts for the year 2012, when the averages "separate". This coincides with the separation of the Sweden price area into four price areas. After 2012 the average actual trade price for quarterly EPADs for Helsinki was above the average actual trade prices for Stockholm for both the trades made through the ETS and OTC. Also for the quarterly contracts the average actual trade price of trades made through the ETS differs from the average actual trade price OTC for both Helsinki and Stockholm.

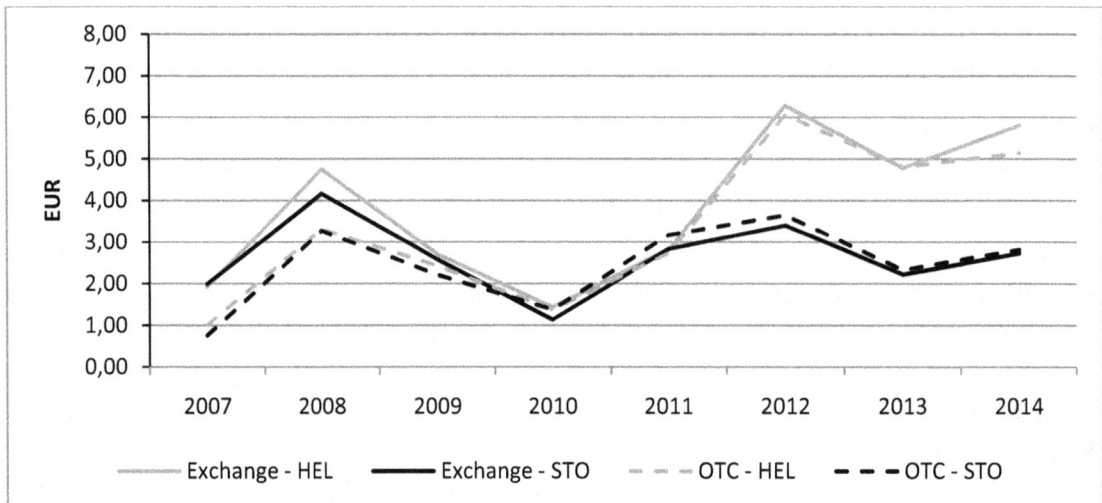

Figure 3.5. Average actual trade price in EUR for quarterly EPAD contracts for Helsinki (HEL) and Stockholm (STO) 2007 – Q1/2014 (for 2014 the data is not complete), separately for trades through the ETS and OTC.

Figure 3.6. shows the average actual trade prices for yearly EPAD contracts for Helsinki and Stockholm for years 2007 – 2014 separately for trades made through the ETS and OTC. The separation of the Sweden price area into four price areas in 2011 is visible also from the chart for yearly average actual trade prices. The average actual trade price for yearly EPADs for Helsinki was above the average actual trade prices for Stockholm for both the trades made through the ETS and OTC for all studied years. Also for the yearly contracts the average actual trade price of trades made through the ETS differs from the average actual trade price OTC for both Helsinki and Stockholm.

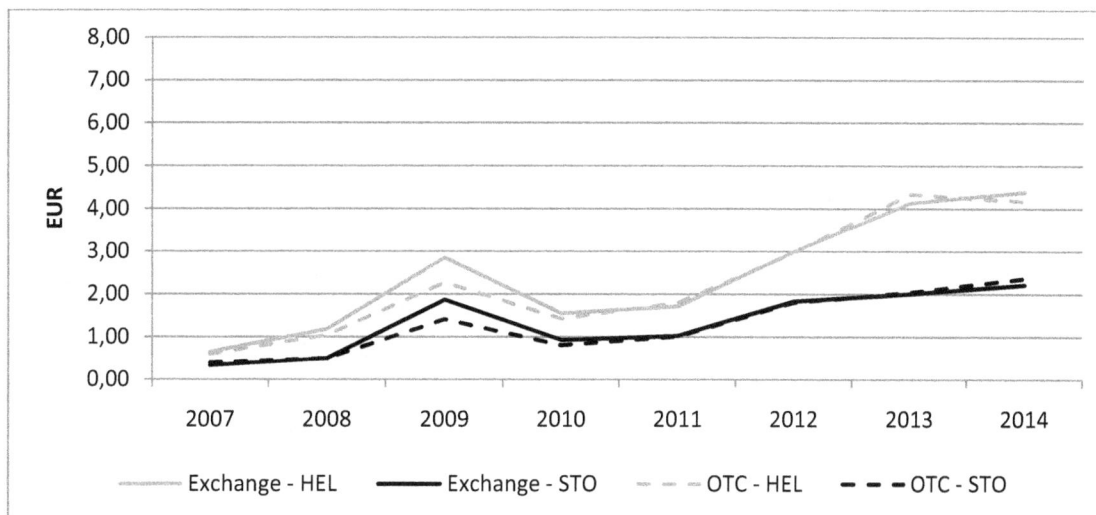

Figure 3.6. Average actual trade price in EUR for yearly EPAD contracts for Helsinki (HEL) and Stockholm (STO) 2007 – 2014, separately for trades through the ETS and OTC.

> **The average actual trade price for yearly contracts was higher for Helsinki than for Stockholm for all studied years for trades through the ETS and OTC.**

3.3. Difference between the average closing price levels of EPAD contracts and the average actual trade price levels

In this section we combine the analyses from sections 3.1. and 3.2. and compare the average closing price levels with the average price levels of actually executed trades through the ETS and OTC for Helsinki.

Figure 3.7. shows the average actual trade price (in EUR) for the trades executed through the ETS and OTC and the average daily closing price (average Daily Fix) for monthly EPAD contracts for Helsinki for the years 2007 – 2014. What can be seen is that the average daily closing price differs from the average actual trade price through the ETS and OTC and for the majority of the years studied the average actual trade price is above the average closing price. The difference in the average daily closing price and the average actual trade price through the ETS varies between 0,02 EUR (2010) and 1,17 EUR (2008), the average difference is 0,57 EUR. The difference in the average daily closing price and the average actual trade price OTC varies between 0,01 EUR (2009) and 1,36 EUR (2010), the average difference is 0,21 EUR.

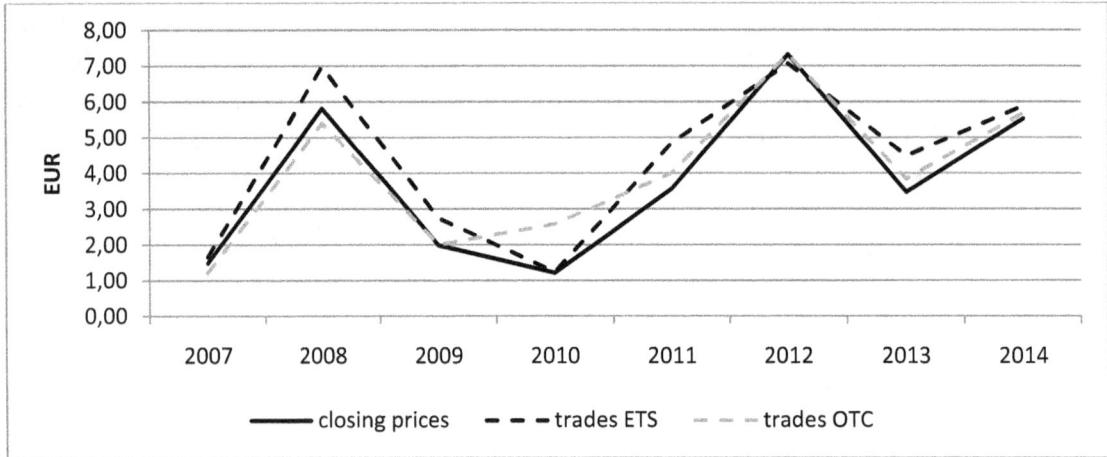

Figure 3.7. Average actual trade price in EUR for trades through the ETS and OTC, and average daily closing prices for monthly EPAD contracts for Helsinki (HEL) for years 2007 – 2014 (2014 data not complete).

Figure 3.8. shows the average actual trade price (in EUR) for the trades executed through the ETS and OTC and the average daily closing price (average Daily Fix) for quarterly EPAD contracts for Helsinki for the years 2007 – 2014. What can be seen is that the average daily closing price differs from the average actual trade price through the ETS and OTC and for the all years studied, except for 2013, the average actual trade prices are above the average closing price. The difference in the average daily closing price and the average actual trade price through the ETS varies between 0,17 EUR (2010) and 2,18 EUR (2008), difference in the average daily closing price and the average actual trade price OTC varies between 0,09 EUR (2009) and 1,06 EUR (2012). The average difference between the average daily closing and average actual trade price through the ETS is 0,83 EUR, and 0,37 EUR between the average daily closing and the average actual OTC trade price.

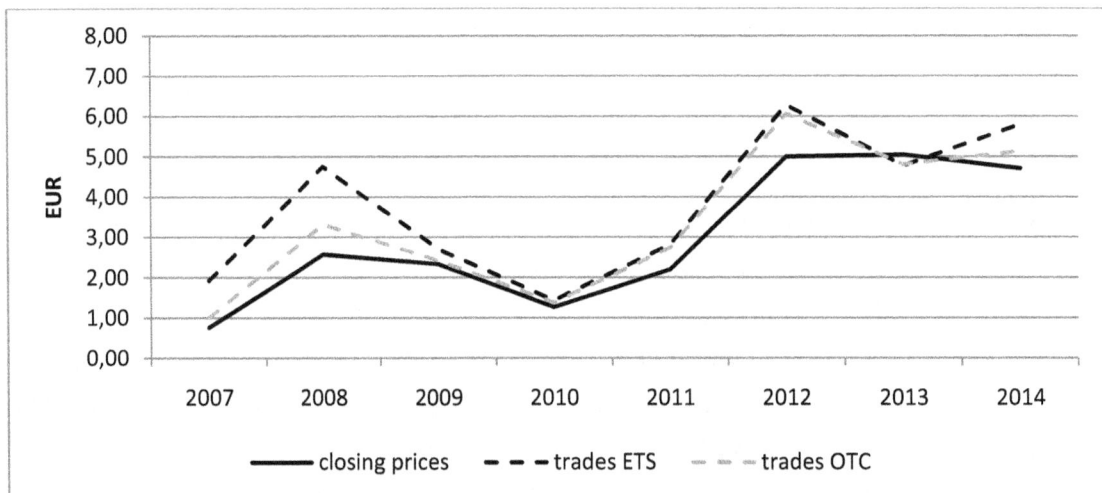

Figure 3.8. Average actual trade price in EUR for trades through the ETS and OTC, and average daily closing prices for Quarterly EPAD contracts for Helsinki (HEL) for years 2007 – 2014 (2014 data not complete).

The average daily closing price differs significantly from the average actual trade prices for most years for monthly and quarterly contracts.

Figure 3.9. shows the average actual trade price (in EUR) for the trades executed through the ETS and OTC and the average daily closing price (average Daily Fix) for yearly EPAD contracts for Helsinki for the years 2007 – 2014. What can be seen is that the average daily closing price has been lower than the average actual trade prices every year for yearly contracts since 2008.

The difference in the average daily closing price and the average actual trade price through the ETS varies between 0,08 EUR (2007) and 1,40 EUR (2009), difference in the average daily closing price and the average actual trade price OTC varies between 0,14 EUR (2007) and 1,23 EUR (2013). The average difference between the average daily closing and average actual trade price through the ETS is 0,63 EUR, and 0,52 EUR between the average daily closing and the average actual OTC trade price.

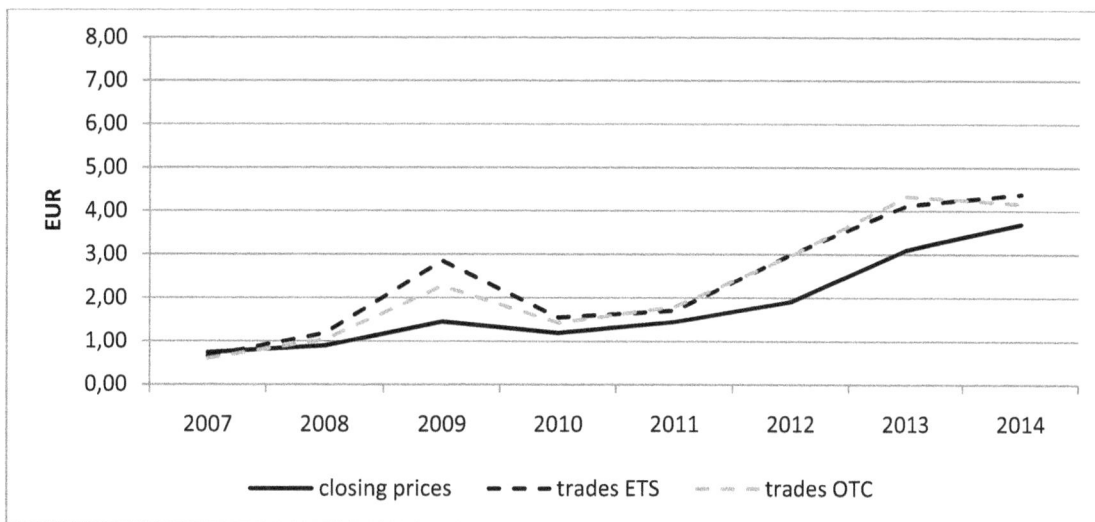

Figure 3.9. Average actual trade price in EUR for trades through the ETS and OTC, and average daily closing prices for yearly EPAD contracts for Helsinki (HEL) for years 2007 – 2014.

> **The average daily closing price has been lower than the average actual trade prices every year for yearly contracts since 2008.**

The fact that there is consistently a considerable difference that seems to vary from year to year between the average actually traded prices and the average daily closing price shows (for all contract maturities) that the average daily closing price (or the daily closing price in general) may not alone be a sufficient yardstick, when one tries to understand the price development of EPAD contracts. We now turn our focus to how the daily closing price (Daily Fix) is determined, to see if we can identify a reason for the differences in the averages discussed above.

3.4. Determination of the daily closing price (Daily Fix) for EPAD contracts

We now turn into looking at how, according to NASDAQ OMX that runs the electronic trading system (ETS) for trading the Nordic EPAD contracts, the closing price (Daily Fix) for EPAD contracts is determined.

A facsimile of the Trading Appendix 2 / Clearing Appendix 2 "Contract Specifications – Commodity Derivatives" issued by NASDAQ OMX Oslo ASA and NASDAQ OMX Clearing AB (Effective date: 20 April 2015) states about the determination of the Daily Fix (daily closing price) for Exchange Listed Products is the following (p. 8-9):

4.4 Daily Fix

4.4.1 The Exchange determines a Daily Fix for each Series on each Bank Day, applying the rules set out below.

4.4.2 The Daily Fix for Exchange Listed Products shall, unless otherwise specified in the Contract Specifications, be the last Exchange Transaction price registered in ETS at a point in time selected at random within the five (5) minutes period specified in the Trading and Clearing Schedule. If this price falls outside the Spread at the time selected, the Daily Fix will be the average of this Spread.

4.4.3 If no Exchange Transactions were registered in ETS the relevant Bank Day, the Daily Fix shall be the average of the Spread registered in ETS at the time selected under Section 4.4.2.

4.4.4 If no Exchange Transactions or Orders are registered, or only buy Orders or only sell Orders were registered in ETS the relevant Bank Day, the Exchange will calculate a theoretical Daily Fix.

4.4.5 In the event of a suspension of ETS lasting the remaining Bank Day, the Exchange may determine a Daily Fix for the Exchange Listed Products in accordance with Sections 4.4.2 - 4.4.4 on the basis of the Orders and Exchange Transactions registered at the time of suspension.

4.4.6 Notwithstanding Sections 4.4.2 - 4.4.5, the Exchange may calculate a theoretical Daily Fix if the Exchange believes that the registered prices or Orders are manipulated or in any other way influenced so that they do not reflect the market value of the Series. The Exchange shall inform the Exchange Members of such events.

Section 4.4.2. stipulates that the daily closing price for EPAD contracts is the price of the last trade made through the ETS system registered on the day at a time that is determined randomly from the time interval 15.55 – 16.00 (CET). In other words, the exchange randomly selects a point of time from the interval, say 15.57.14 (fourteen seconds past 15.57 CET) and checks what was the last registered trade price made through the ETS system that day, and sets that as the daily closing price. Any trades after that time and before the close of trading do not count in determining the daily closing price.

In case the selected last trade price falls outside the spread (outside the price area between the best bid price and the best ask price) at the (randomly selected) selection time, the daily closing price will be the average of the best ask price and the best bid price. In other words, if the last trade has happened, for example, in the first hour of trading at the price 1,00 EUR and at the (randomly selected) selection time the best bid price is above 1,00 EUR or the best ask price is below 1,00 EUR the daily closing price will be the average of the average of the best ask price and the best bid price.

Section 4.4.3. stipulates that the closing price will be the average of the best bid price and the best ask price registered in the ETS at the time selected under section 4.4.2 if there are no trades made through the ETS system during the trading day.

A theoretical closing price (theoretical Daily Fix) is calculated by the exchange and becomes the closing price, if there are no exchange transactions registered (there is no last trade price for the day) and a spread cannot be determined (because a best bid price, a best ask price, or both are missing).

In practice these stipulations may mean, for example, the following:

a. If there are no trades made through the ETS during a trading day the closing price is determined as the average of the best ask price and the best bid price (at the time the closing price is determined)

b. If there are trades made OTC (and visible through the ETS) during the trading day, but there are no trades made through the ETS, the closing price is determined as the average of the best ask price and the best bid price (at the time the closing price is determined)

c. If there are no trades made through the ETS during a trading day and a best bid price, a best ask price, or both are missing a theoretical closing price is calculated and becomes the closing price

d. If there are trades made OTC (and visible through the ETS) during the trading day, but if there are no trades made through the ETS during a trading day and a best bid price, a best ask price, or both are missing a theoretical closing price is calculated and becomes the closing price.

The above examples illustrate possible reasons behind why the average daily closing prices for different contract maturities differ from the average actually traded prices. The daily closing price (Daily Fix) does not involve the information contained in any trades OTC.

> **The daily closing price (Daily Fix) does not include the information contained in any trades OTC.**

3.5. Volatility of EPAD contract prices

Volatility tells us how much the value of an observed variable changes on average during a specific time period. Volatility is commonly measured by using standard deviation. Standard deviation of prices in EUR is also a EUR figure, we are more interested in how many percent the price volatility is – for this we need to have a benchmark, from which the percentage is calculated. For this purpose we use the average daily closing price.

The standard deviation is calculated by using all contracts of the same maturity with delivery on the year in question. This means that any seasonal variations and / or possible cycles are "lost" in the analysis. The same procedure is used for both analyzed price areas Stockholm and Helsinki. The results obtained are general and direction giving, for more detailed results single contracts should be analyzed separately and, for example, per contract average standard deviations calculated.

The procedure for calculating the standard deviation as a percentage of the average daily closing price is simple: we divide the absolute standard deviation (in EUR) by the average daily closing price (in EUR) and multiply by 100%. We do this for selected price areas for different contract maturities for contracts for years 2007 – Q1/2014.

Figure 3.10. shows the volatility of monthly EPAD contracts as a percent of the daily closing price for Helsinki and Stockholm for 2007 – 2014 (2014 data is not complete). One can see that the volatility is different for different years and changes in the observation period are dramatic. There is also a difference in the volatility between Helsinki and Stockholm. Volatilities of over 100% of the average closing price are observed.

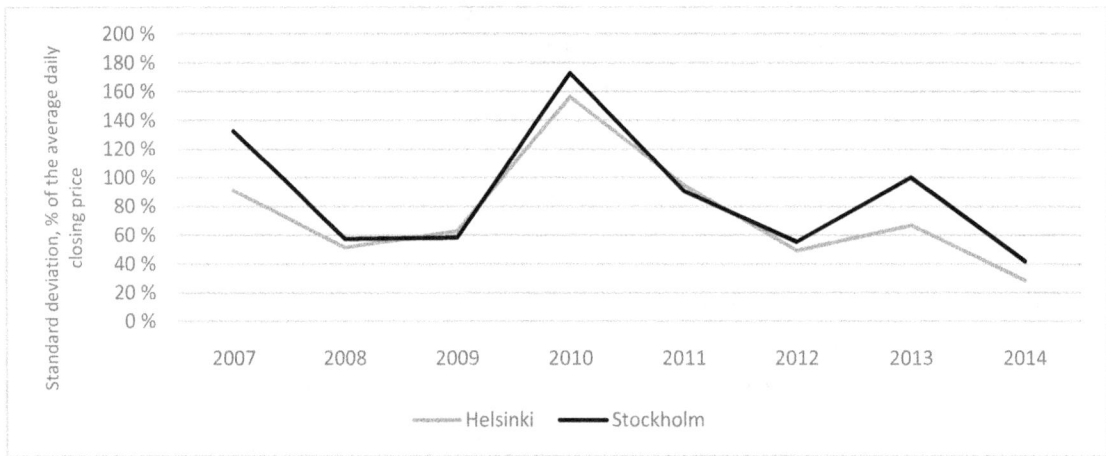

Figure 3.10. Standard deviation as a percent of the average daily closing price for monthly EPAD contracts for Stockholm (STO) and for Helsinki (HEL) for contracts with delivery 2007 – 2014 (data for 2014 not complete)

Figure 3.11. shows the volatility of quarterly EPAD contracts as a percent of the daily closing price for Helsinki and Stockholm for 2007 – 2014 (2014 data is not complete). One can see that the volatility is different for different years and changes in the observation period are dramatic. There is also a difference in the volatility between Helsinki and Stockholm.

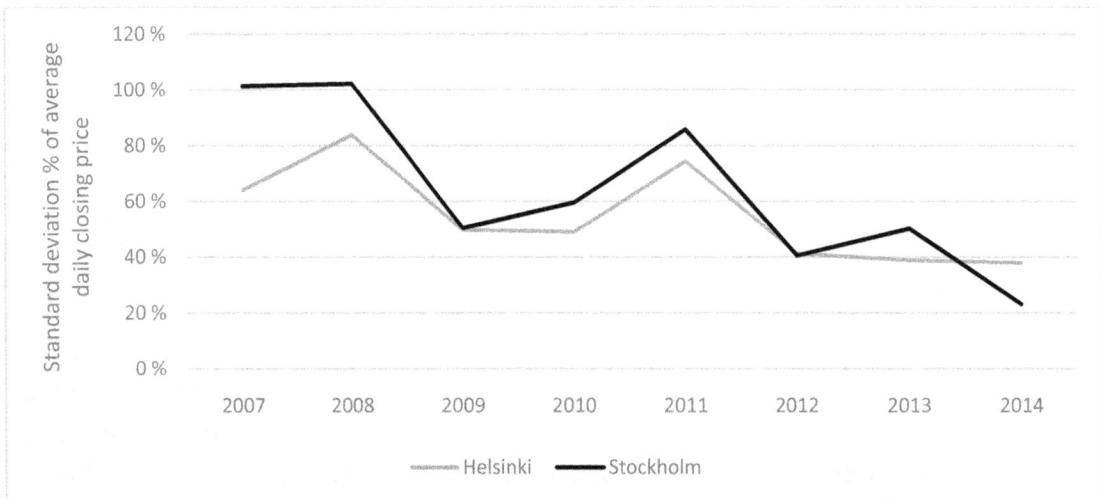

Figure 3.11. Standard deviation as a percent of the average daily closing price for quarterly EPAD contracts for Stockholm (STO) and for Helsinki (HEL) for contracts with delivery 2007 – 2014 (data for 2014 not complete)

Figure 3.12. shows the volatility of yearly EPAD contracts as a percent of the daily closing price for Helsinki and Stockholm for 2007 – 2014. One can see that the volatility is different for different years and changes in the observation period are dramatic. There is also a difference in the volatility between Helsinki and Stockholm.

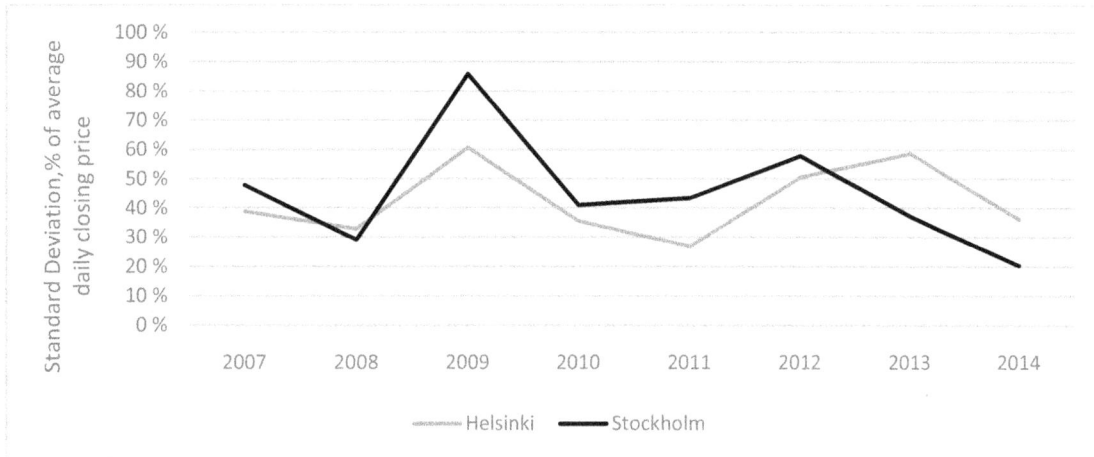

Figure 3.12. Standard deviation as a percent of the average daily closing price for yearly EPAD contracts for Stockholm (STO) and for Helsinki (HEL) for contracts with delivery 2007 – 2014

For all maturities the volatilities observed are above 20% for all observed years. The highest volatilities are recorded in connection with the monthly contracts (maximum of 175% of the average closing price is recorded for Stockholm in 2010). All in all volatilities of contracts with all maturities change dramatically from year to year.

> **Volatilities of contracts with all maturities change dramatically from year to year.**

4. EPAD contract price spread

Spread is the difference between the best bid price (buy order price, the price a buyer is willing to pay) and the best ask price (sell order price, the price a seller is willing to sell for) present in a marketplace, in the case of EPAD trade the electronic trading system (ETS). In other words, the spread tells how far apart the "selling side" view of the price of an EPAD is from the "buying side" view of the same EPAD.

If a market participant wants to buy a contract, the best ask price is the lowest available price on the ETS for which the contract can be bought. Similarly, if a market participant wants to sell a contract, the best bid price is the highest available price on the ETS for which the contract can be sold. The spread is how much an intra-day, "first buy, then sell"-operation on a single contract would cost in terms of the difference between the best buying and the best selling price obtainable on the ETS.

In this section we study the spreads of the EPAD markets:

First, we look at the average level of spreads in terms of money (absolute) for each contract maturity (montly, quarterly, and yearly) for contracts with delivery on different years for selected price areas Stockholm (STC) and Helsinki (HEL).

Second, we look at the average level of spreads in terms of how many percent of the *ask price* the spreads are on average for each contract maturity for contracts with delivery on different years for the same selected price areas. This is a conservative way of calculating the spread as a percentage, because the ask price is the "upper level" of the spread and therefore, when it is used as the divisor the spread as a percentage will certainly not be overstated.

Third, we look at the spreads of some selected single EPAD contracts for Helsinki and Stockholm price areas in detail.

4.1. Average bid-ask spreads for the selected price areas (in absolute money terms)

We calculate the spread by dividing the sum of differences between the best ask and the best bid price, divided by the number of days n in the sample, see formula (1).

$$Average\ absolute\ bid-ask\ spread\ =\ \frac{\sum(best\ ask - best\ bid)}{n} \tag{1}$$

The calculations are made for contracts on different years in the way that for a yearly contract that points to a delivery during the year 2008 the spread will have been calculated from during the trading time of that contract, before 2008. The same logic applies for contracts of a shorter maturity. Days for which both, a bid and an ask price exist have been taken into consideration in the calculations.

Figure 4.1. shows the average spreads for monthly EPAD contracts with delivery in years 2007 - 2013 for the selected price areas. The average spread seems to change from year-to-year for both price areas. The highest average spread for both price areas was for 2008 contracts (1,12 EUR for STO and 1,19 EUR for HEL). For the contracts for 2013 the average absolute spreads were 0,69 EUR for Stockholm and 0,72 EUR for Helsinki.

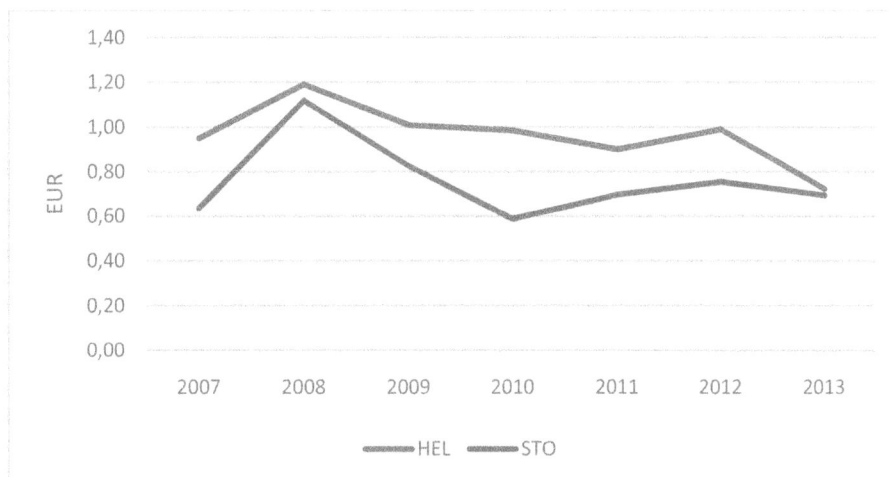

Figure 4.1. Average spread in EUR for monthly EPAD contracts for 2007 – 2013 for the selected price areas.

The average absolute spread for Helsinki is higher than for Stockholm for all studied years. The difference is highest for the year 2010 (0,40 EUR).

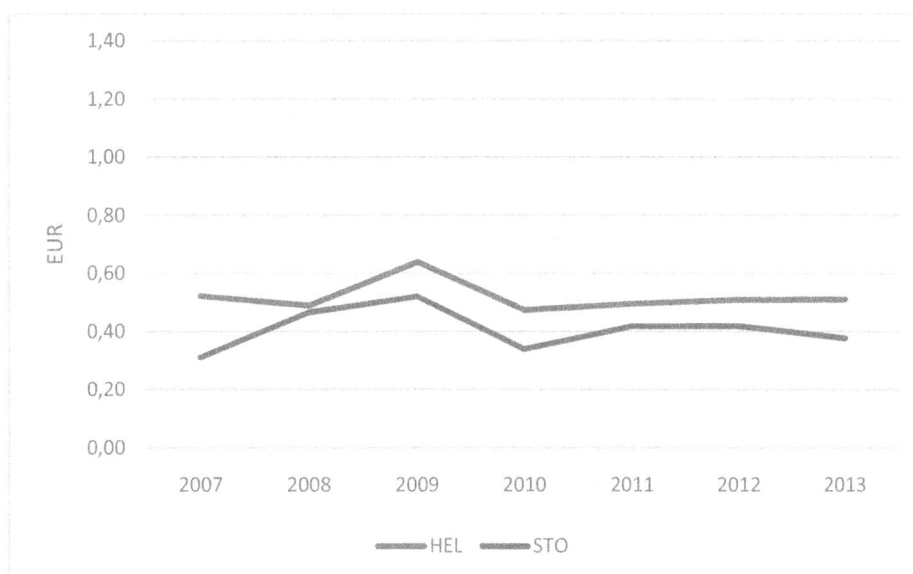

Figure 4.2. Average spread in EUR for quarterly EPAD contracts for the selected price areas 2007 - 2013.

Figure 4.2. shows the average absolute spreads for quarterly contracts for the years 2007 – 2013. The overall level of the average spreads is considerably lower than for monthly contracts. The highest average spread for both price areas was for 2009 contracts (0,52 EUR for STO and 0,64 EUR for HEL). The average absolute spread for Helsinki is higher than for Stockholm for all studied years.

Figure 4.3. shows the average absolute spreads for quarterly contracts for the years 2007 – 2013. The overall level of the average spreads is considerably lower than for monthly contracts. The highest average spread for both price areas was for 2007 contracts and has come down to remain at an under 0,50 EUR level for Helsinki and at an under 0,40 EUR level for Stockholm.

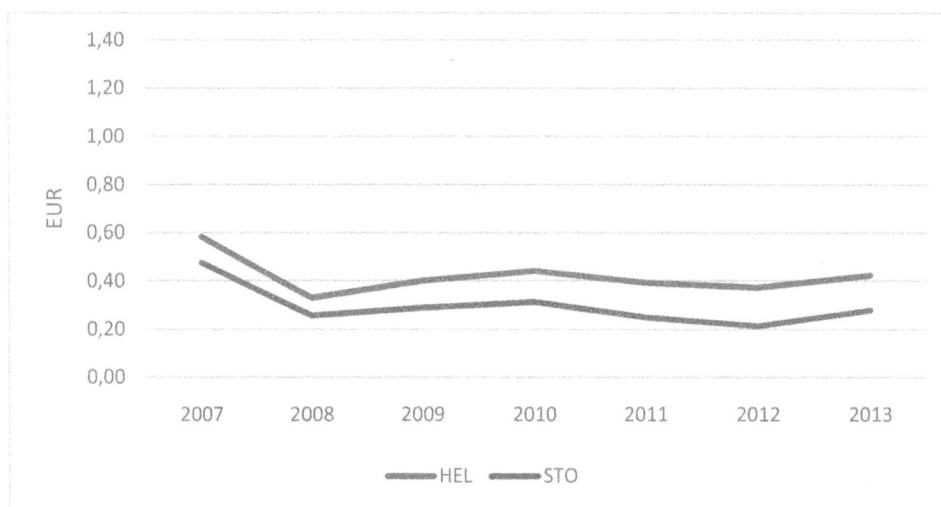

Figure 4.3. Average spread in EUR for yearly EPAD contracts for the selected markets 2007 - 2013.

The average absolute spread for Helsinki is higher than for Stockholm for all studied years. The difference between the average absolute spreads in Helsinki and Stockholm after 2009 has remained in between 0,10 and 0,15 EUR.

> **The average absolute spread for Helsinki is higher than for Stockholm for all studied years for all contract maturities.**

4.2. Average spread as a percentage of the best ask price

We calculate the daily percentage spread as the difference between best ask and best bid price divided by the best ask price. The average percentage spread is calculated by dividing the sum of daily percentage spreads by the number of days n in the sample, see formula (2).

$$Average\ spread\ as\ a\ \%\ of\ the\ best\ ask\ price = \frac{\Sigma\left(\frac{best\ ask - best\ bid}{best\ ask} * 100\%\right)}{n} \tag{2}$$

The calculations are (again) made for contracts in terms of the year the delivery takes place. Days for which both, a bid and an ask price exist have been taken into consideration in the calculations.

Figure 4.4. shows the development of the average spread as a percentage of the best ask price for monthly EPAD contracts for years 2007 – 2013. It is clear from the figure that the average spread as a percentage has varied rather wildly during the observation period. For Helsinki the minimum is 13,1% (2012) and the maximum 99,3% (2010), for Stockholm the minimum is 23,7% (2008) and the maximum 80,6% (2013).

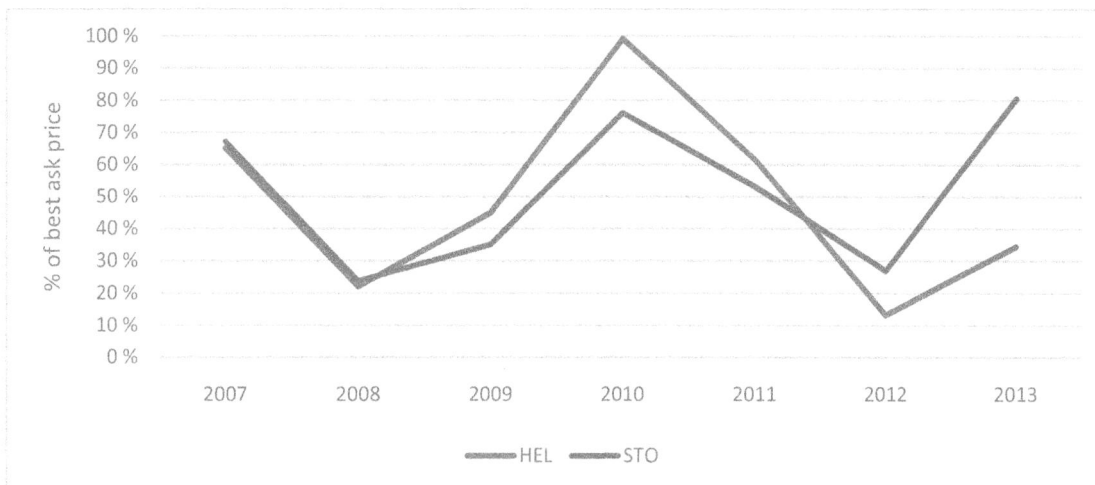

Figure 4.4. Average spread as % of the best ask price for monthly EPAD contracts for the selected markets 2007 - 2013.

Figure 4.5. shows the average spread as a percentage of the best ask price for quarterly EPAD contracts for years 2007 – 2013. For Helsinki the minimum is 11% (2012) and the maximum 58% (2007), for Stockholm the minimum is 14,8% (2012) and the maximum 48,8% (2007).

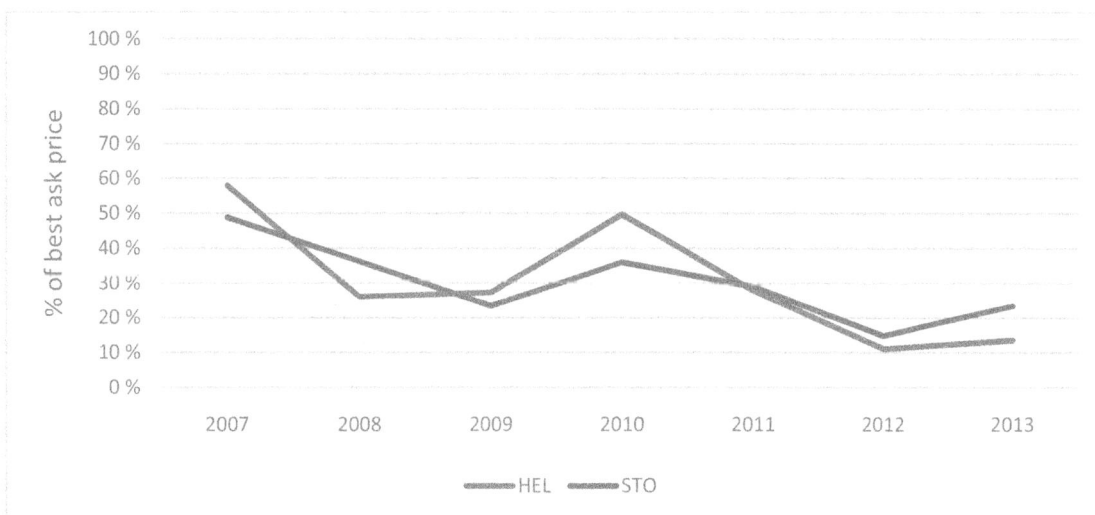

Figure 4.5. Average spread as % of the best ask price for quarterly EPAD contracts for the selected markets 2007 - 2013.

> **The average spread as a percentage of the best ask price has changed from year to year for all contract maturities.**

The average spread as a percentage of the best ask price of the quarterly contracts has changed from year to year, however the variance has been lower than the variance of the monthly contracts´ average spreads as a percentage of the best bid price.

Figure 4.6. shows the average spread as a percentage of the best ask price for yearly EPAD contracts for years 2007 – 2013. The percentage spread has been calculated from the only (one) relevant contract for each year. The spreads for Helsinki and Stockholm follow a similar path and there seems to be a downward trend in the size of the spreads.

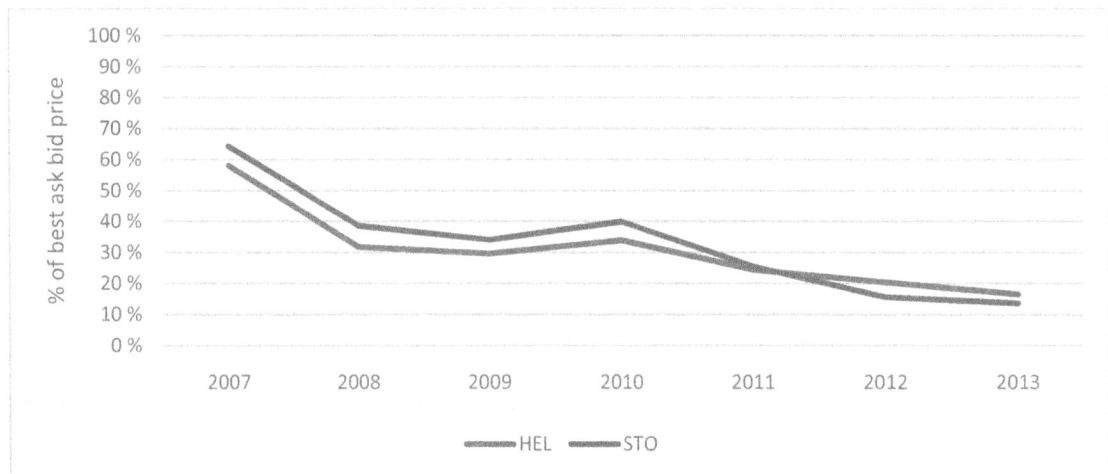

Figure 4.6. Average spread as % of the best ask price for yearly EPAD contracts for the selected markets 2007 - 2013.

For contracts with delivery on the year 2008 and later the average percentage spread has remained between 10% - 40% for both Stockholm and Helsinki. For contracts with delivery on 2013 the average percentage spreads were 16,5% for Helsinki and 13,6% for Stockholm.

All in all, looking at the average spreads as a percentage of the best ask price for all contract maturities one can note that the average percentage spread is for all years at an over 10% level.

> **The average spread as a percentage of the best ask price is for all years at an over 10% level.**

4.3. Spread of selected single EPAD contracts

In this section we look specifically at selected EPAD contracts´ spread and study in more detail how the size of the spread develops during the contract trading period in absolute EUR terms and in terms of percentage of the best ask bid price. We have selected two contracts for this purpose, a yearly contract for Stockholm 2013 (SYSTOYR-13) and a monthly contract for Helsinki for March 2013 (SYSHELMAR-13).

Figure 4.7. shows the closing price and spread data for the trading period of the SYSTOYR-13 yearly contract. The trading time starts in the beginning of 2010 and is three years. There were 743 days for which the spread could be determined during the trading period and the average spread was 0,278 EUR and the average spread as a percentage of the best ask bid price was 13,6%.

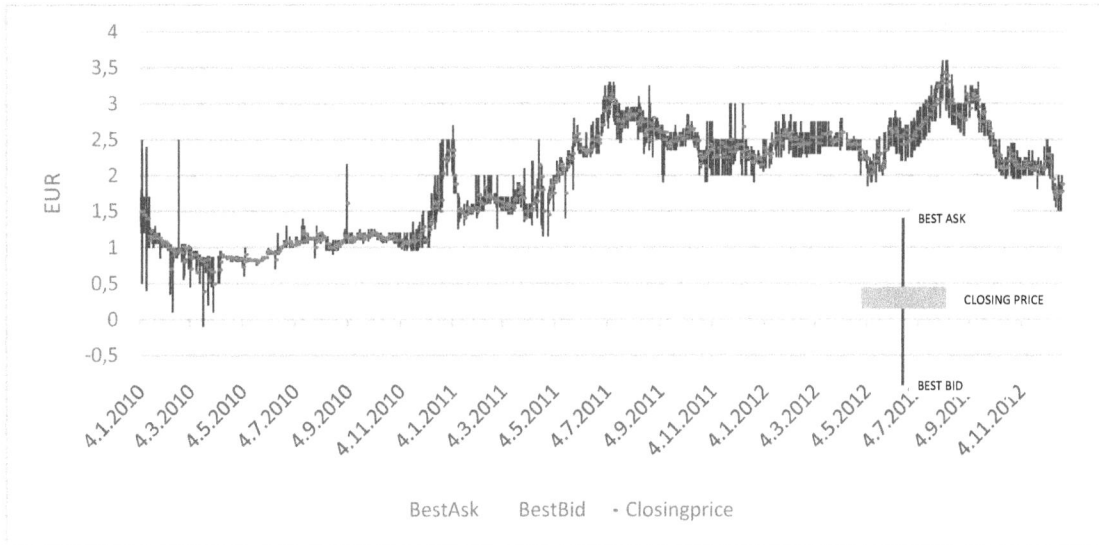

Figure 4.7. Closing price data for the trading period of Stockholm yearly EPAD for 2013 (SYSTOYR-13), with the best bid and the best ask prices (spread) for each day indicated.

Figure 4.8. shows the daily spread in EUR for the SYSTOYR-13 contract, for the whole trading period of the contract. The daily spread in EUR varies rather a lot during the trading period, the highest spread observed is 2,00 EUR and the lowest spread 0,01 EUR. The mode is 0,25 EUR (the most frequently occurring value) that occurs 69 times or slightly over 9% of the trading days.

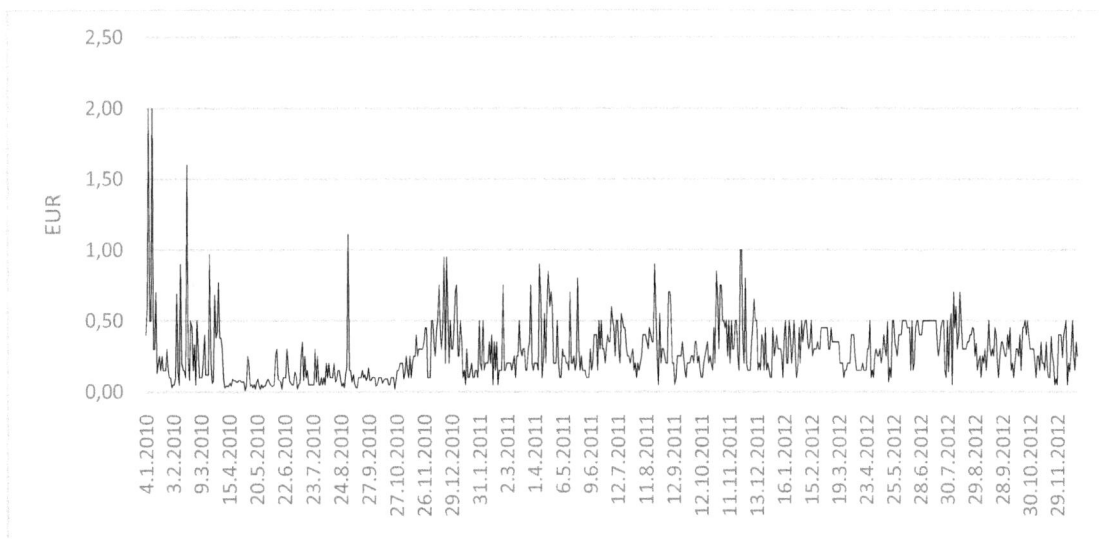

Figure 4.8. Absolute daily spread in EUR for SYSTOYR-13 trading time.

The daily spread in EUR varies rather a lot during the trading period

Figure 4.9. shows the daily spread as a percentage of the best ask bid price for the SYSTOYR-13 contract, for the whole trading period of the contract. The highest percentage spread observed is 111,49% of the best ask price and the lowest percentage spread 1,16% of the best ask price.

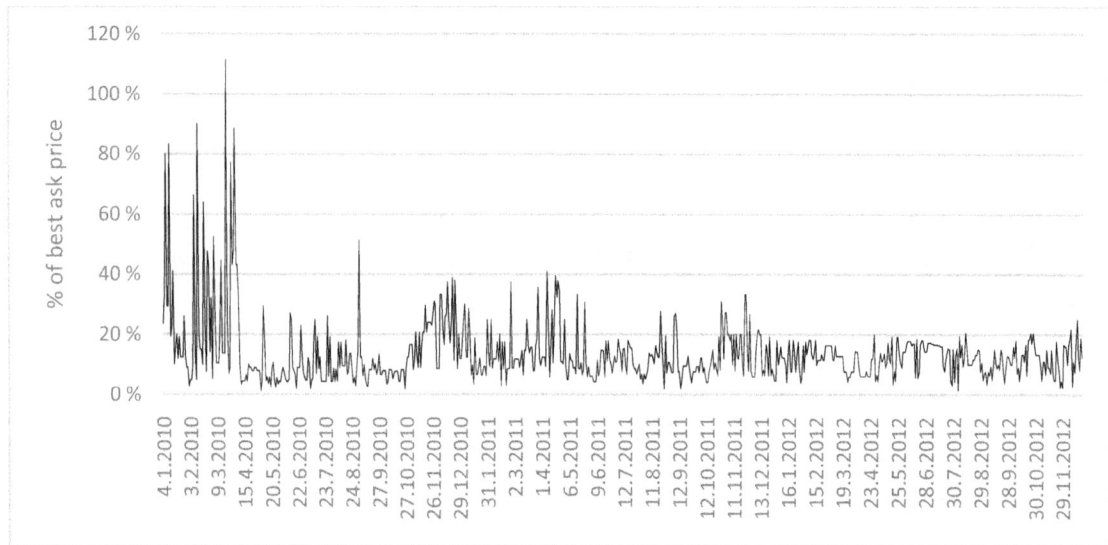

Figure 4.9. Daily spread in % of the best ask price for SYSTOYR-13 trading time.

> **Also the daily spread as a % of the best ask bid price varies during the trading period**

All the highest percentage spreads (over 60%) occurred during the first three months of the trading period.

Figure 4.10. shows the closing price and spread data for the trading period of the SYHELMAR-13 monthly contract for March 2013 for Helsinki. The trading time starts on the 26th of November 2012 and lasts until the end of February 2013. There were 64 days for which the spread could be determined during the trading period and the average spread was 0,65 EUR and the average spread as a percentage of the best ask bid price was 19,6%.

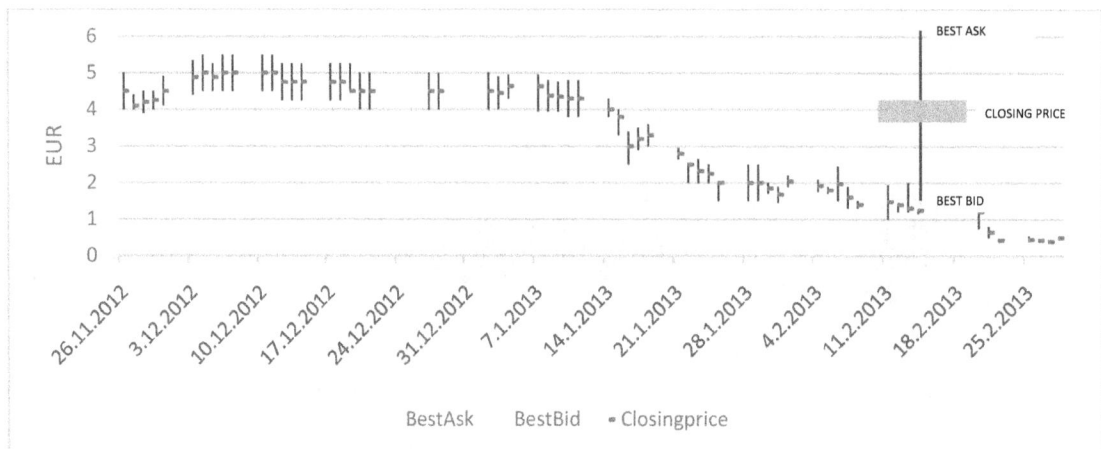

Figure 4.10. Closing price data for the trading period of Helsinki Monthly EPAD for March 2013 (SYHELMAR-13), with the best bid and the best ask prices (spread) for each day indicated.

Figure 4.11. shows the daily spread in EUR for the SYHELMAR-13 contract, for the whole trading period of the contract. The daily spread varies during the trading period, the highest spread observed is 1,00 EUR and the lowest spread 0,05 EUR. The mode is 1,00 EUR (the most frequently occurring value) that occurs 21 times or on slightly under 33% of the trading days.

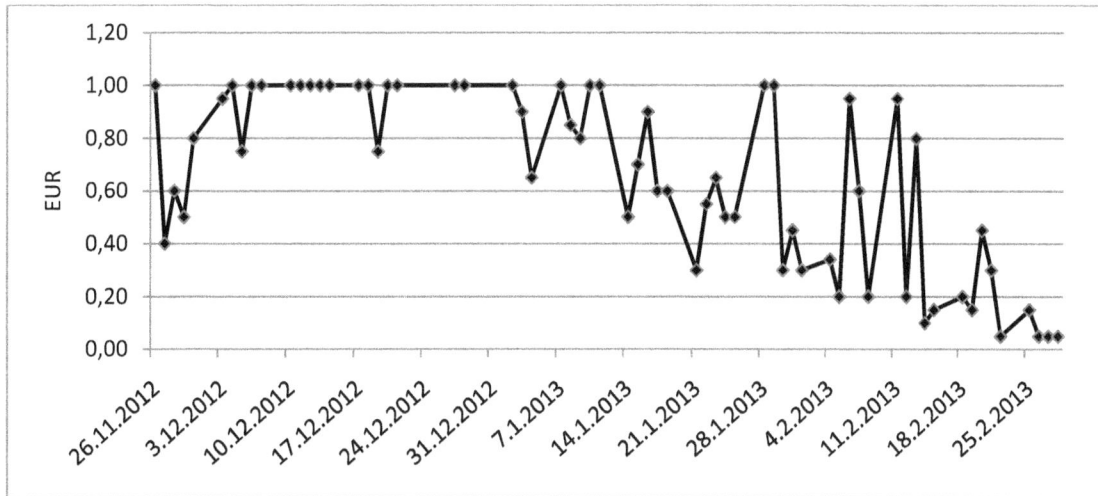

Figure 4.11. Absolute daily spread in EUR for SYHELMAR-13 trading time. Markers show the 64 data points.

The mode of the spread in EUR is 1,00 EUR and it occurs on 21 / 64 trading days, or on slightly under 33% of the trading days.

Figure 4.12. shows the daily spread as a percentage of the best ask bid price for the SYHELMAR-13 contract, for the whole trading period of the contract. The highest percentage spread observed is 48,72% of the best ask price and the lowest percentage spread 8,00% of the best ask price.

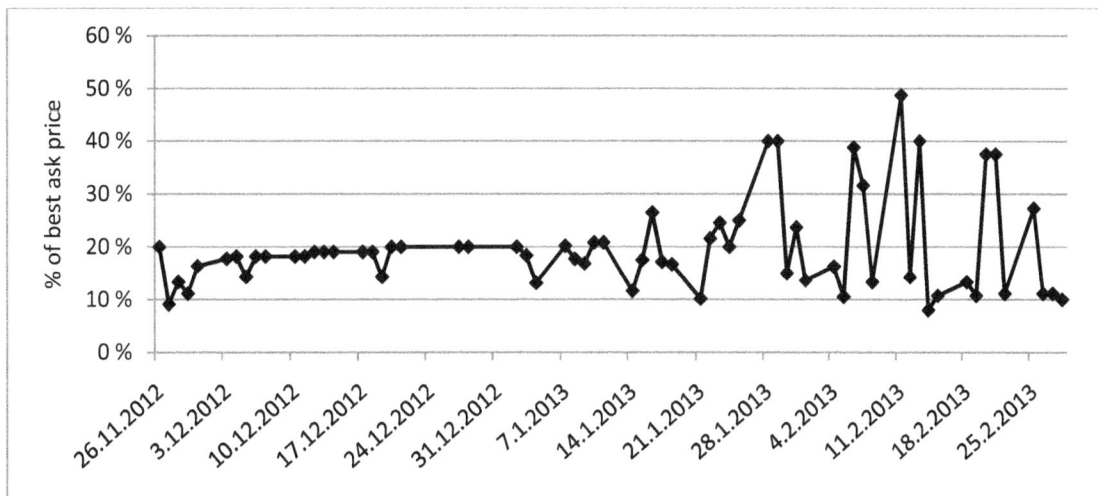

Figure 4.12. Daily spread as % of the best ask bid price for SYHELMAR-13 trading time.

Also the daily spread as a % of the best ask bid price varies during the trading period

5. Market Activity

In this section we investigate the market activity of EPAD contracts by looking at overall and average descriptive yearly numbers about the trades realized. We look, for example, at the number of trades made through the electronic trading system (ETS) and OTC, the traded volumes, and the volume per trade. We look at the Nordic markets overall and also take a look at Finland more specifically.

5.1. Number of trades

The overall number of realized trades tells something about the overall EPAD market activity. Changes in the number of trades realized may indicate changes in market activity or changes in the size of the average volume per trade. It is interesting to compare the number of realized trades through the ETS and OTC, the comparison tells about the structure of the EPAD markets and about the importance of the ETS in the trading in relation to trade OTC.

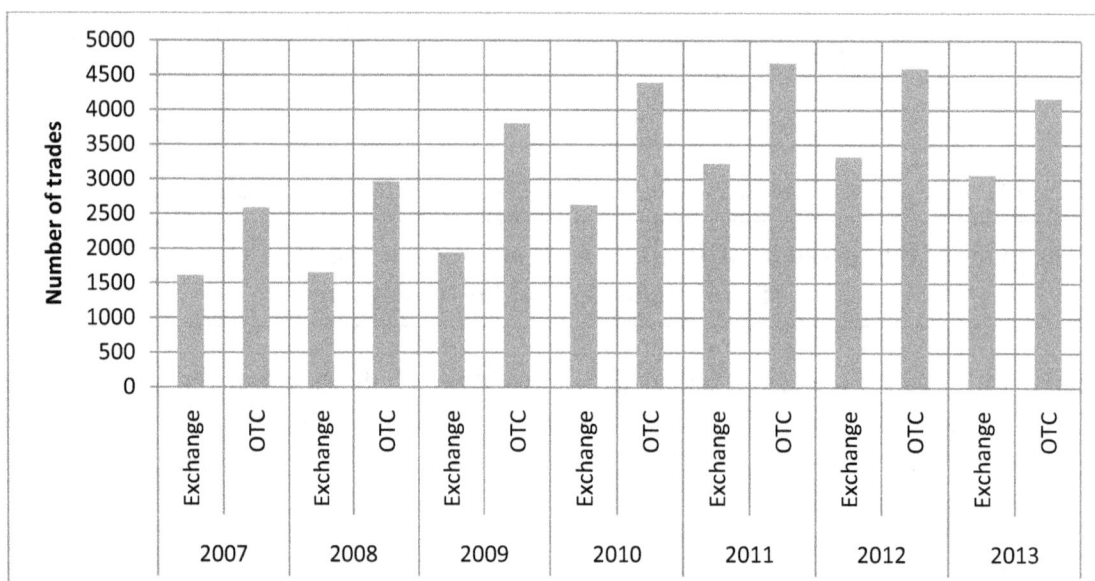

Figure 5.1. Cumulative EPAD trades (all contract maturities) for a given year's contracts through the ETS and OTC cumulative for all price areas for years 2007 – 2013 (overall Nordic data)

Figure 5.1. shows how the number of EPAD trades has developed in the years 2007 - 2013. The most trades overall (7920) were done on contracts for the year 2012. The highest number of OTC trades were made on 2011 contracts and the highest number of trades through the ETS on 2012 contracts. Most trades overall were made on the Stockholm (STO) price area, but after 2013 Helsinki (HEL) has been the largest price area measured by the number of trades.

There have been more trades OTC, than through the ETS on all years' contracts since the year 2007.

> **More trades have been registered OTC than through the ETS for every year 2007 – 2013.**

5.2. Number of contracts traded

Number of trades tells about the absolute number of deals struck, however in each trade a number of contracts are normally traded. Each contract's size is 1MW. In this section we are interested in the descriptive numbers for the number of each year's EPAD contracts traded. Number of contracts traded may be a more reliable indicator of the size of the EPAD markets than the number of trades. In addition to the contracts traded overall, we look at the number of contracts traded OTC and through the ETS.

We also look at the number of contracts traded for the different EPAD products (monthly, quarterly, and yearly). Typically a monthly EPAD consists of between 672 and 744 hours, a quarterly EPAD of between 2159 and 2209 hours, and a yearly EPAD of between 8760 and 8784 hours. A contract's exact size equals the contract volume multiplied by the hours in the contract.

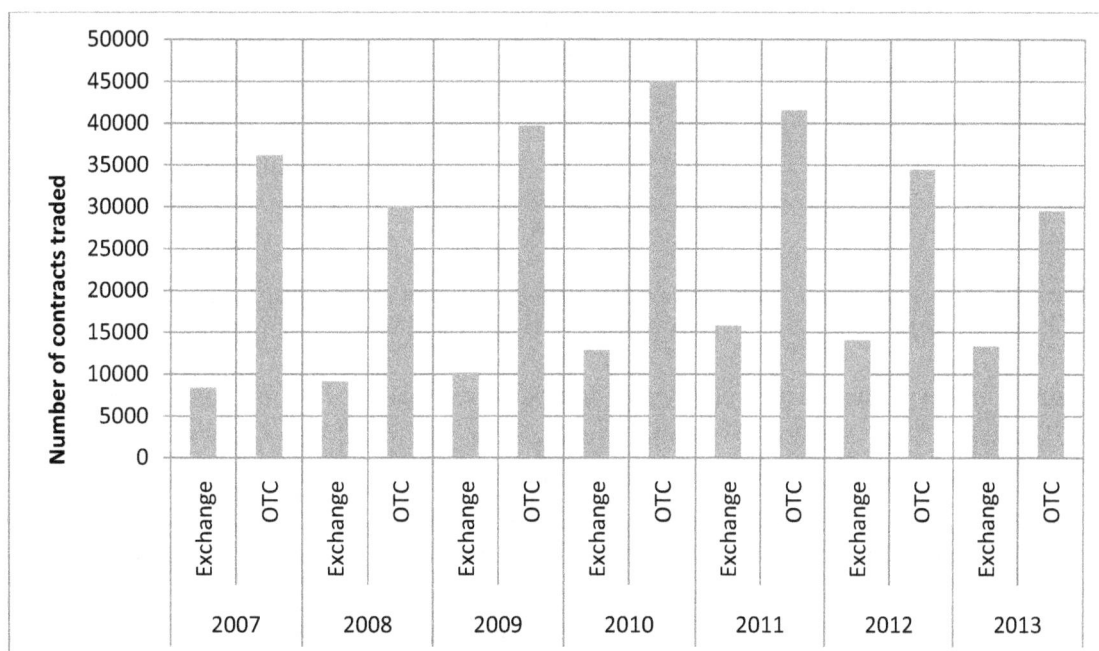

Figure 5.2. Number of contracts traded for each year through the ETS and OTC for years 2007 – 2013, data cumulative for all trading areas (overall Nordic data)

Figure 5.2. shows how the number of contracts traded has developed since the year 2007. The most contracts were traded overall for the year 2010 (57957). For year 2011 the overall number of contracts traded is very close to the number of contracts traded in 2010. In aggregate, more contracts were traded OTC for every year than through the ETS. Of the total number of contracts traded overall (340422,9) approximately 75% were traded OTC (256601,9) and 26% through the ETS (83821).

> **OTC trade accounted for 75% of all contracts traded for 2007 - 2013.**

Having the information on number of trades and on the number of contracts traded allows us to calculate the average number of contracts per trade. We do this separately for each contract type (monthly, quarterly, and yearly) and distinguish between OTC and deals through the ETS.

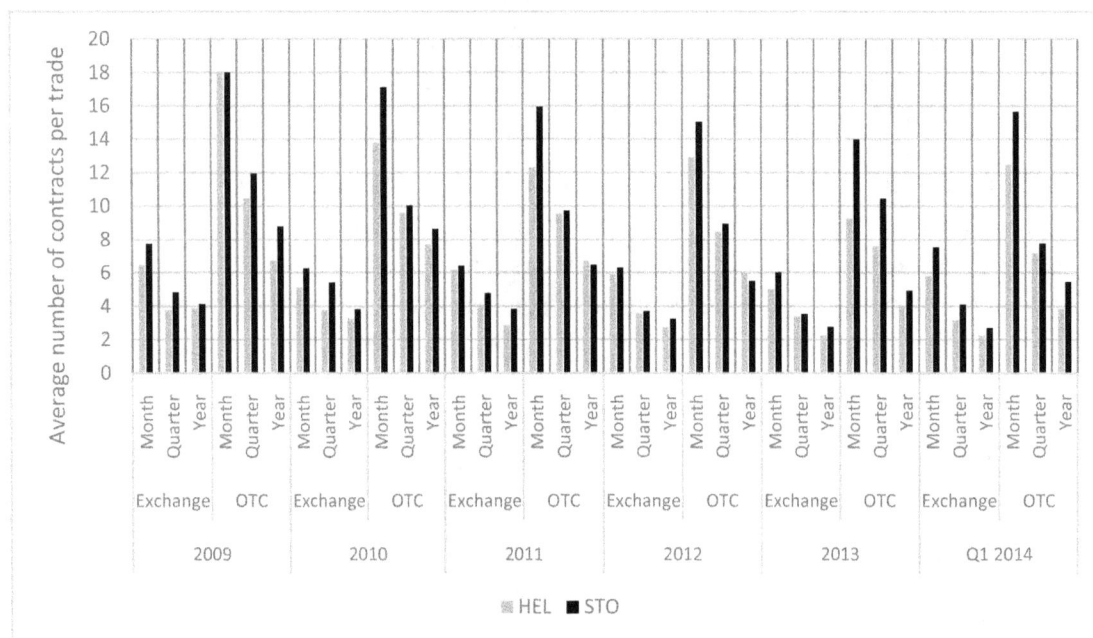

Figure 5.3. Average number of contracts per deal in Helsinki (HEL) and Stockholm (Sweden, before 2011) (STO), breakdown by contract type, contract year, and through the ETS and OTC.

Figure 5.3. shows the average number of contracts per deal for Helsinki and Stockholm for years 2009 – 2013 and for Q1/2014. Average deal size in Stockholm was larger for all contract types, for trades through the ETS and OTC, and for all years with the single exception of yearly contracts through OTC for 2012. On average the number of monthly contracts traded per deal was the largest, followed by the number of quarterly contracts per deal, and the lowest for yearly contracts per deal. One needs to remember that a contract with a longer delivery period hedges a larger volume that is, one yearly contract has approximately the same volume as twelve monthly contracts.

The number of contracts per trade is on average higher in OTC deals than in deals made through the ETS. The difference is most remarkable with regards to monthly contracts.

5.3. Volume turnover

Volume turnover, or the volume traded in TWh, is calculated by multiplying the number of contracts traded with the underlying contract size. The volume information does not tell anything about the motivation for trading that is, possible speculative trading is also included in the figures.

Figure 5.4. shows the cumulative volume of all contracts traded for each year 2007 – 2013. The largest volume turnover was reached in 2010 (172 TWh), after which the volume has come down to 124 TWh in 2013. Measured by traded volume Helsinki and Stockholm are the most important price areas. In 2013 Helsinki and Stockholm accounted for over 71% of the overall volume.

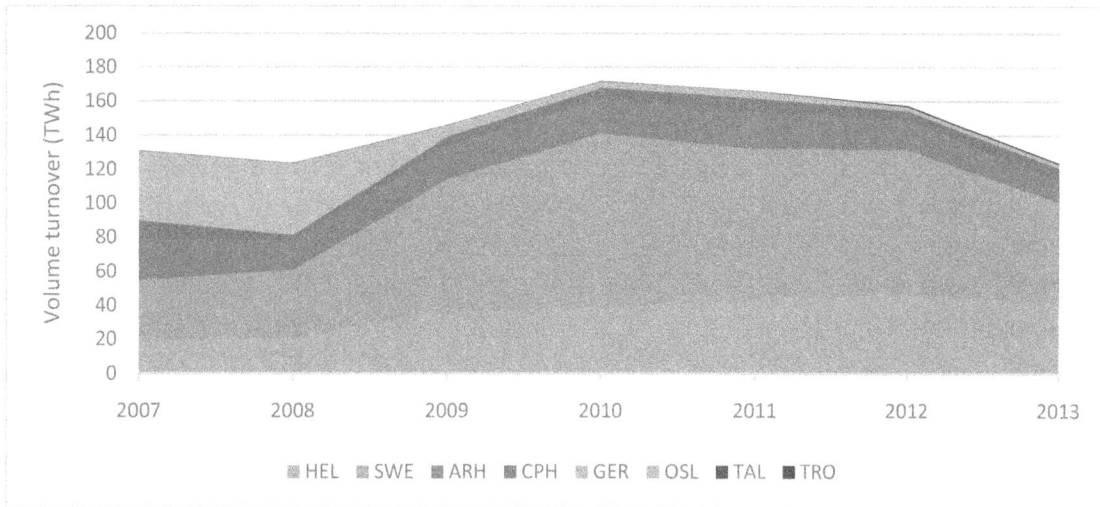

Figure 5.4. Volume turnover (TWh) for years 2007 – 2013, cumulative for all price areas including volume traded OTC and through the ETS for all contract maturities. All Swedish price areas cumulated in to SWE.

Measured by traded volume Helsinki and Stockholm are the most important price areas.

Figure 5.5. displays the percentage share of the overall volume (all contract maturities cumulated) traded through the ETS and OTC. The portion of the overall trading volume traded through the ETS is approximately 20% for years 2007 to 2013. In other words, eighty percent of the overall Nordic traded EPAD volume for years 2007 - 2013 was traded OTC. This situation has remained rather stable around 20%, while the total volume traded has dropped since 2010.

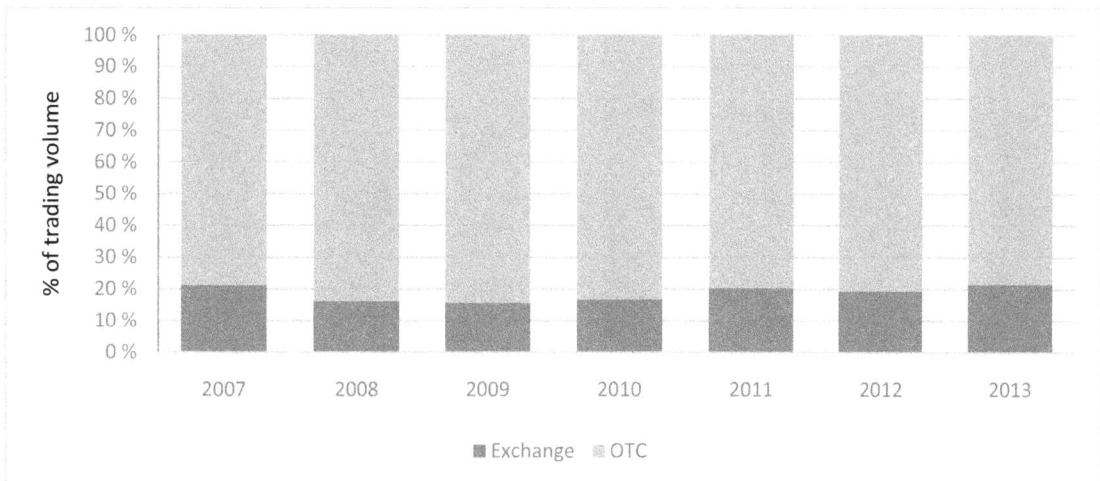

Figure 5.5. The share of the overall volume traded through the ETS and OTC in percent 2007 – 2013 including all contract types.

Around eighty percent of the overall volume is traded OTC

Yearly contracts account for the majority of the overall volume traded for all years, totalling over 60% of the overall volume every year between 2010 and 2013, and over 50% for the years 2007 - 2009. Clear majority of the yearly contracts' volume is traded OTC.

> **Yearly contracts account for the majority of the overall traded volume.**

Next we look at how the trading volume is distributed between trades made through the electronic trading system and OTC for Helsinki, in Sweden, and in Århus to find out how volume is distributed inside these trading areas. Sweden here means Stockholm for years 2006 – 2010 and the composite of Stockholm (STO), Luleå (LUL), Malmö (MAL), and Sundsvall (SUN) for 2011 – Q1/2014. Sweden was split into four price areas in 2011.

Figure 5.6. shows the total volume and the distribution of traded volume for Helsinki (HEL) between the ETS and OTC. The total volume was highest for contracts for the year 2012 (47,9 TWh). For each one of the years 2007 – 2013 more than 85% of the Helsinki total volume was traded OTC.

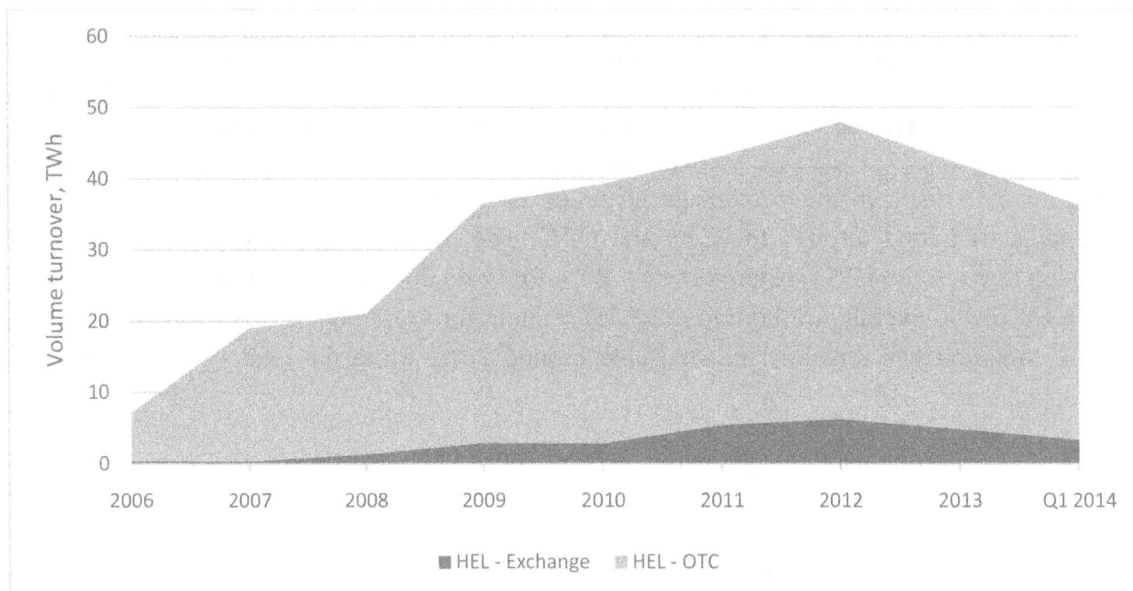

Figure 5.6. Total volume traded (TWh) through the ETS and OTC for Helsinki. (2006 and 2014 not full data)

> **For each one of the years 2007 – 2013 more than 85% of the Helsinki total volume was traded OTC.**

Figure 5.7. shows the total volume traded for Sweden and the distribution of the traded volume between ETS and OTC. Total volume peaked for the contracts for the year 2010 (102 TWh). The volume traded for Sweden through the ETS has remained under 20% for contracts on all years between 2007 and 2013, and reaching over 18% in 2013.

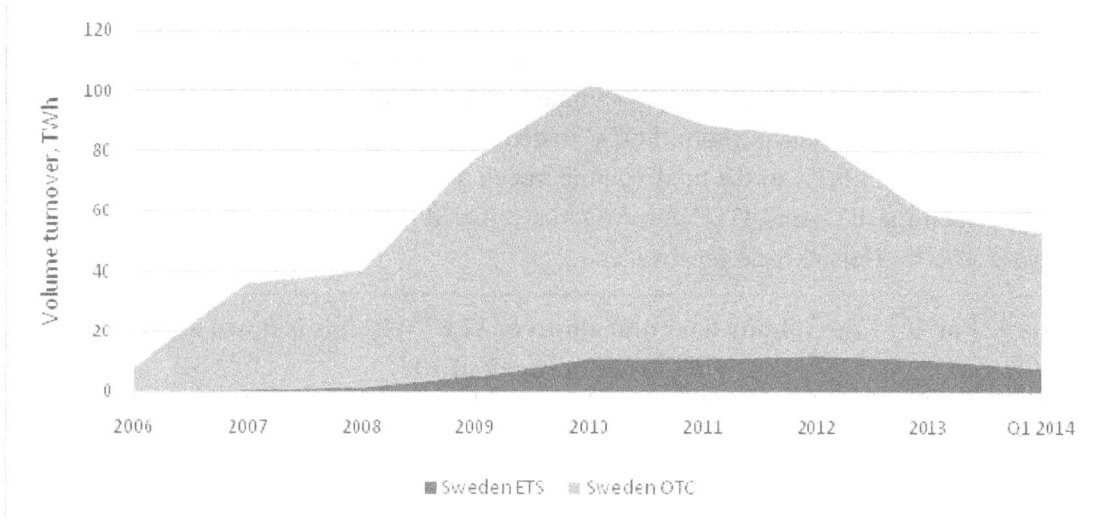

Figure 5.7. Total volume traded (TWh) through the ETS and OTC for Sweden. (2006 and 2014 not full data)

The overall traded volume for Sweden has decreased from the peak in 2010, from 102TWh to 59TWh in 2013. This is a remarkable decrease of over 40TWh in contracted volume.

> **The overall traded volume for Sweden has decreased from the peak in 2010, from 102TWh to 59TWh in 2013.**

Figure 5.8. shows the total volume traded for Århus (ARH) and the distribution of the traded volume between ETS and OTC. The total overall volume peaked in 2007 at 24TWh and dropped in 2008 only to go up again in 2009 – 2011 to over 20TWh. For 2013 the volume has come down to 12,6TWh, this is down almost 50% from the peak of 2007.

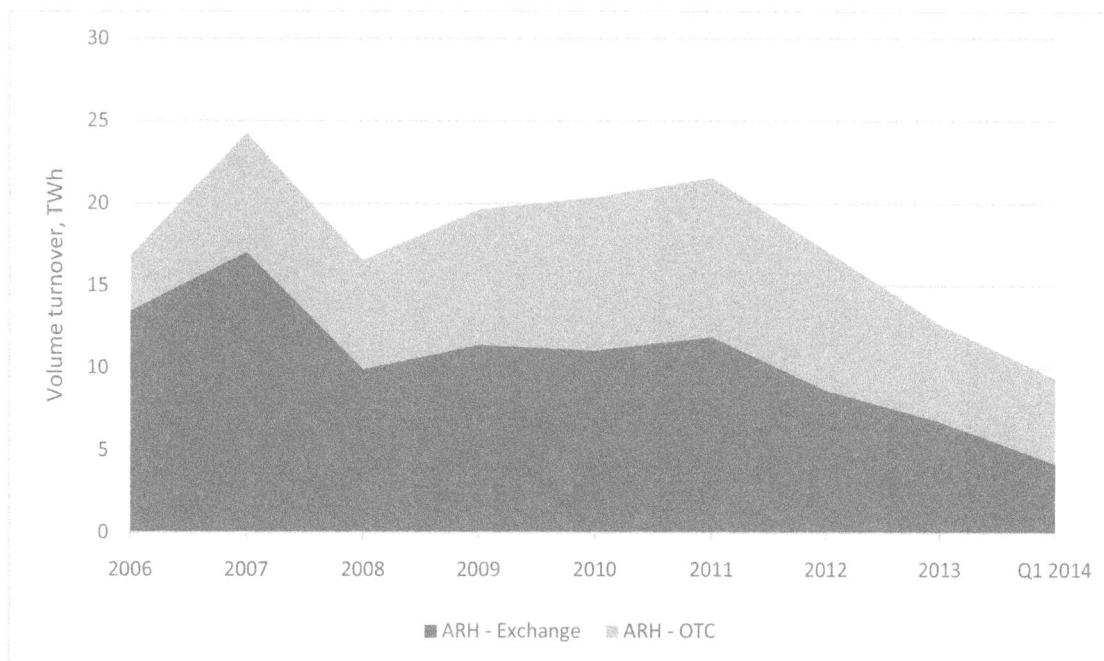

Figure 5.8. Total volume traded (TWh) through the ETS and OTC for Århus. (2006 and 2014 not full data)

The volume traded for Århus through the ETS has remained over 50% for contracts on all years between 2007 and 2013. For 2007 contracts the OTC accounted for little under 30% of the volume and in 2012 the portion of OTC traded volume peaked at just under 50%. In 2013 OTC accounted for 46,7% of the total volume traded in Århus. The distribution of the volume traded through the ETS and OTC for Århus is rather different from the distribution of the volume traded for Helsinki and for Sweden.

For 2013 the volume has come down to 12,6TWh, this is down almost 50% from the peak of 2007.

PART III

Illustrative Cases

6. CASE 1: Helsinki monthly EPAD for May 2013 (SYHELMAY-13)

In this section and the following two sections, we present cases of selected EPAD contracts and investigate the question "what does the trading period of a typical contract look like?". In this first case, we study a monthly EPAD for May 2013 Helsinki, code SYHELMAY-13, a contract whose trading started on the 2nd of January 2013 and ended on the 30th April 2013. During the trading period there were 82 trading days.

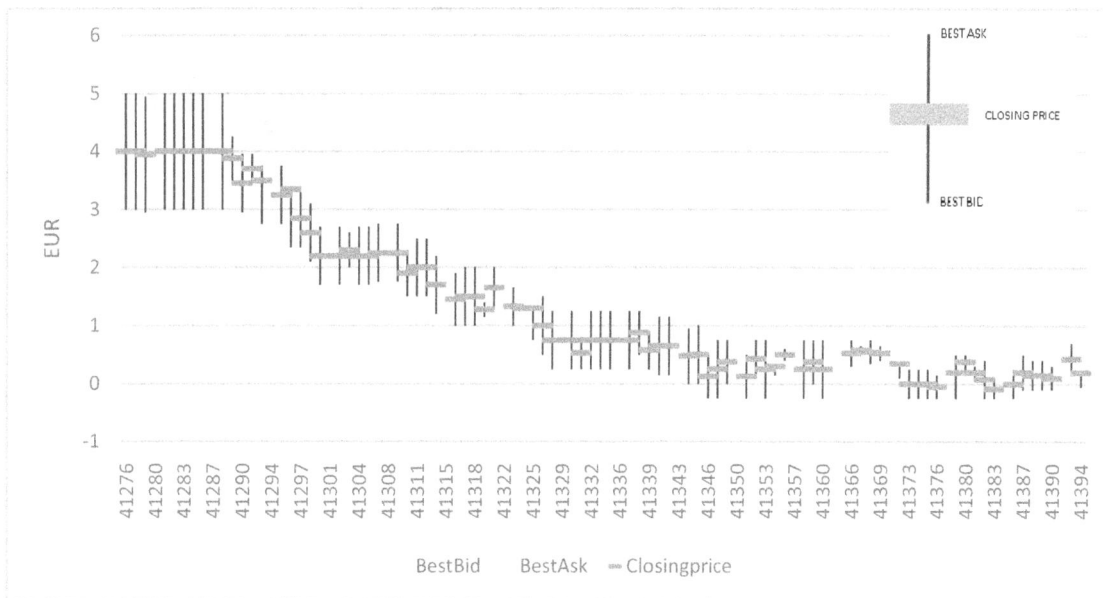

Figure 6.1. Closing price data for the trading period of Helsinki monthly EPAD for May 2013 (SYHELMAY-13), with the best bid and the best ask prices.

Figure 6.1. above shows the price development of the SYHELMAY-13 EPAD contract. Difference between the daily best ask and the best bid quotes is the spread of the bids registered on the electronic trading system. From Figure 6.2., it can be observed that in the beginning of the trading time the spread is exactly 2 euro for some time and then drops to a lower level. On 31 trading days the spread is exactly 1 euro.

> **It is evident that the spread does not remain constant throughout the trading period.**

The maximum observed spread is 2 euro and the minimum spread 0,10 euro. It is evident that the spread does not remain constant throughout the trading period.

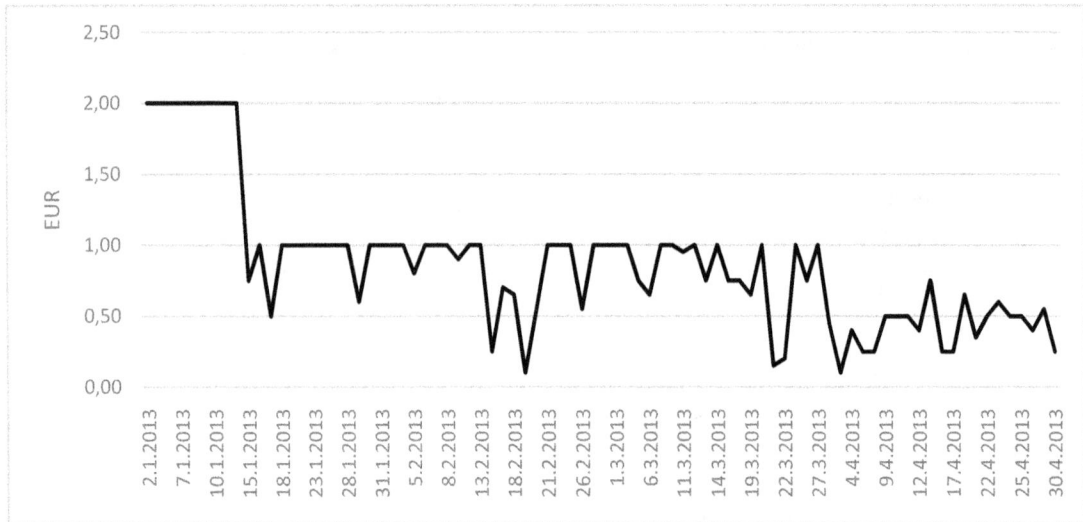

Figure 6.2. Spread in EUR for the trading period of Helsinki monthly EPAD for May 2013 (SYHELMAY-13)

On average the spread is 0,86 EUR, which corresponds to an average daily spread of 77,9% of the best bid price.

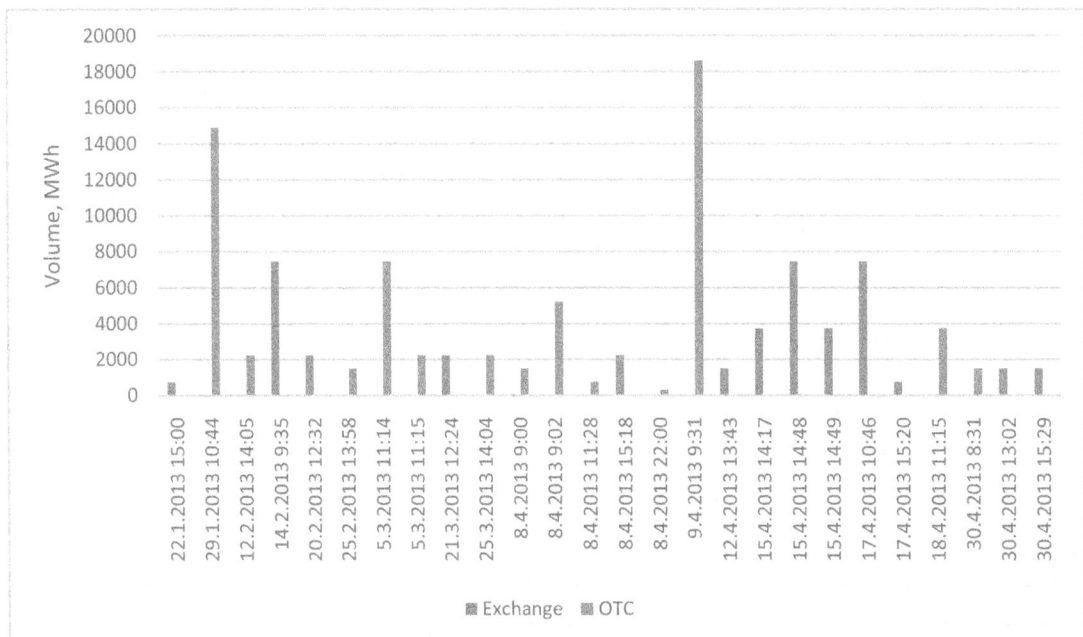

Figure 6.3. Volumes traded on the electronic trading system (ETS) and over the counter OTC during the trading period of Helsinki monthly EPAD May 2013 (SYHELMAY-13)

Figure 6.3., shows the trading volumes of the SYHELMAY-13 contract for the trades conducted through the electronic trading system and over the counter. The overall trading volume through the ETS is 42408 MWh and 62049,6 MWh OTC, the total number of trades is 26 and consists of thirteen trades through both the ETS and OTC. The two largest trades have taken place OTC. More than half, sixteen, of all trades took place in April, the final month of the contract trading time.

> **The trading volume OTC is larger than through the ETS.**

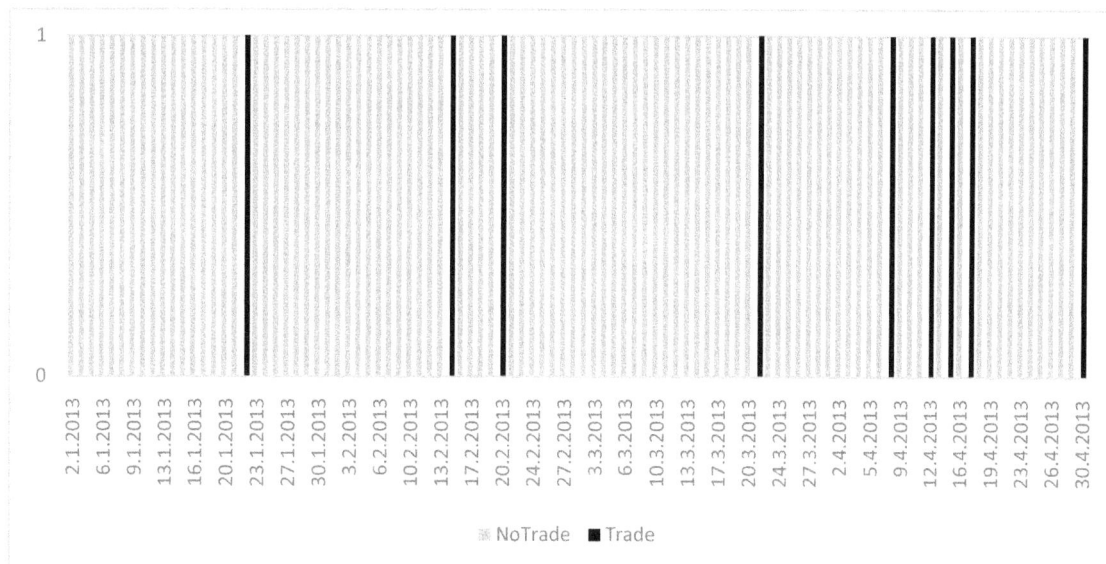

Figure 6.4. Days with and without trade through the ETS during the trading period of Helsinki monthly EPAD May 2013 (SYHELMAY-13)

Figure 6.4. illustrates the days with trade vs. the days without trade through the electronic trading system. Of the 82 trading days during the trading time of the SYHELMAY-13 contract there is at least one trade through the electronic trading system on nine trading days, or just under 11% of all trading days. The closing price of the SYHELMAY-13 contract has been determined as an average of the best sell and best ask bids 73 out of 82 trading days and on nine days the closing price has been determined by actual trades.

> **There is at least one trade through the ETS on nine trading days, or just under 11% of all trading days.**

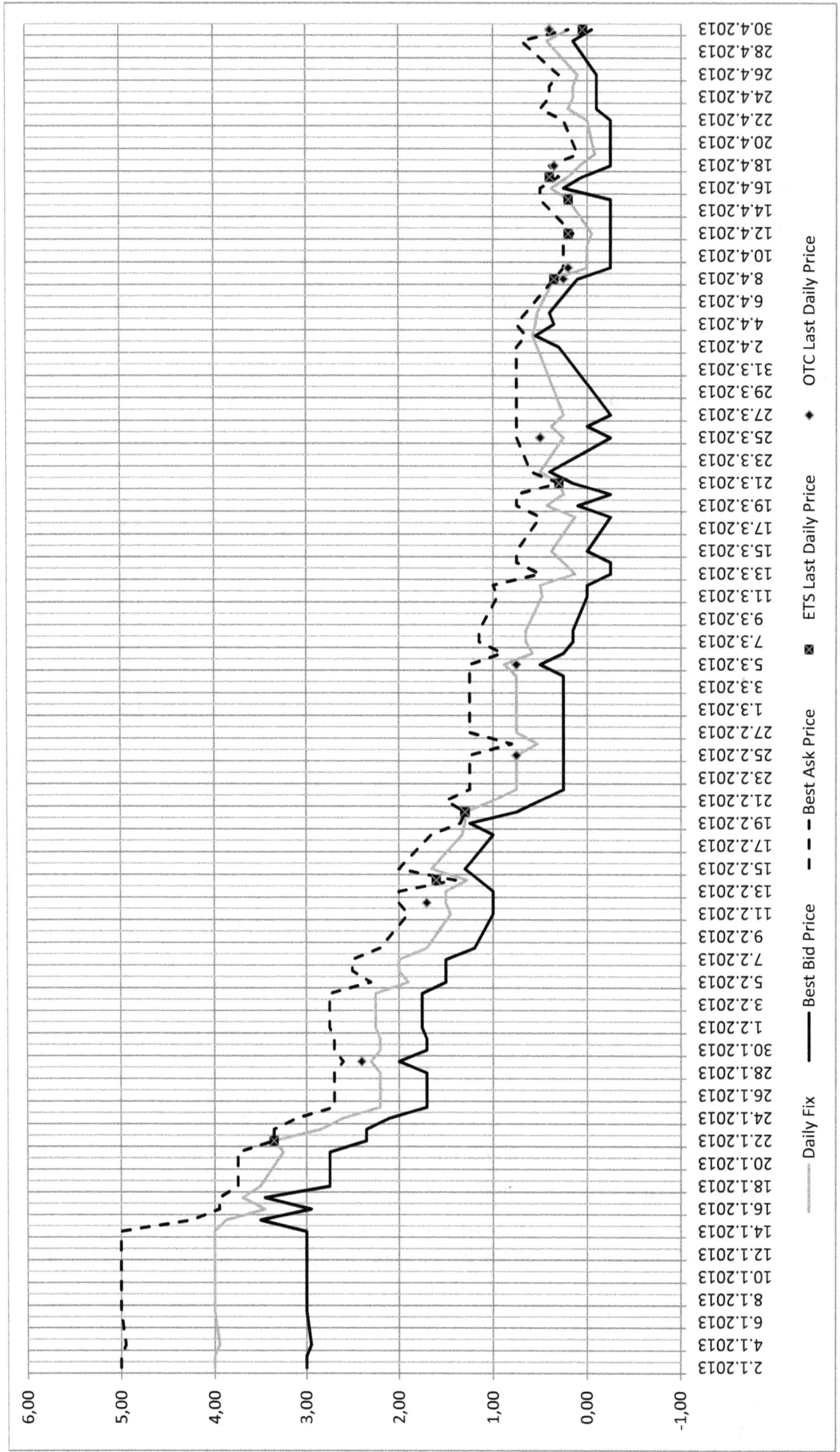

Figure 6.5. The figure shows the trading time for a monthly EPAD contract for Helsinki for May 2013 (SYHELMAY-13). Visible are the daily closing price (Daily Fix), the daily best ask price, the daily best bid price, and the last actually traded daily price for OTC and through the ETS separately.

7. CASE 2: Stockholm monthly EPAD for May 2013 (SYSTOMAY-13)

In this second case, we study a monthly EPAD for May 2013 Stockholm (Sweden area 3), code SYSTOMAY-13, a contract whose trading started on the 2nd of January 2013 and ended on the 30th April 2013. During the trading period there were 82 trading days. The idea is to give a possibility to compare monthly contracts on two areas.

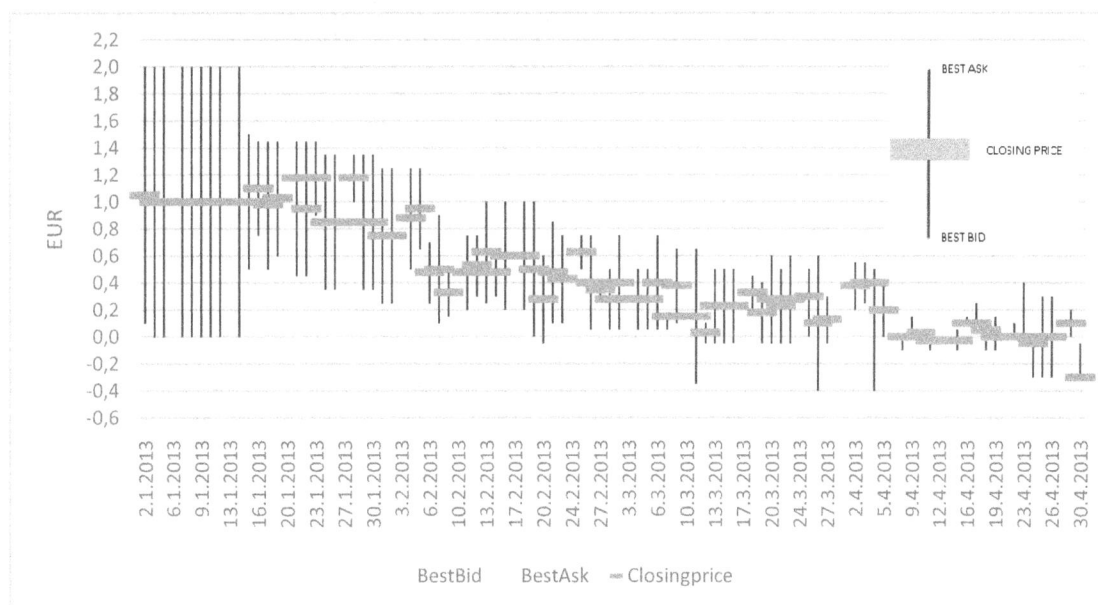

Figure 7.1. Closing price data for the trading period of Stockholm monthly EPAD for May 2013 (SYSTOMAY-13), with the best bid and the best ask prices.

Figure 7.1. above shows the price development of the SYSTOMAY-13 EPAD contract. The difference between the daily best ask and the best bid quotes is the spread of the bids registered on the electronic trading system, the development of the absolute spread (spread in EUR) for the trading period of the contract is visible in Figure 7.2. Also here it can be observed that in the beginning of the trading time the spread is exactly 2 euro for some time and then drops to a lower level. In the beginning of the trading period the size of the spread is double the closing price.

> **In the beginning of the trading period the size of the spread is double the closing price.**

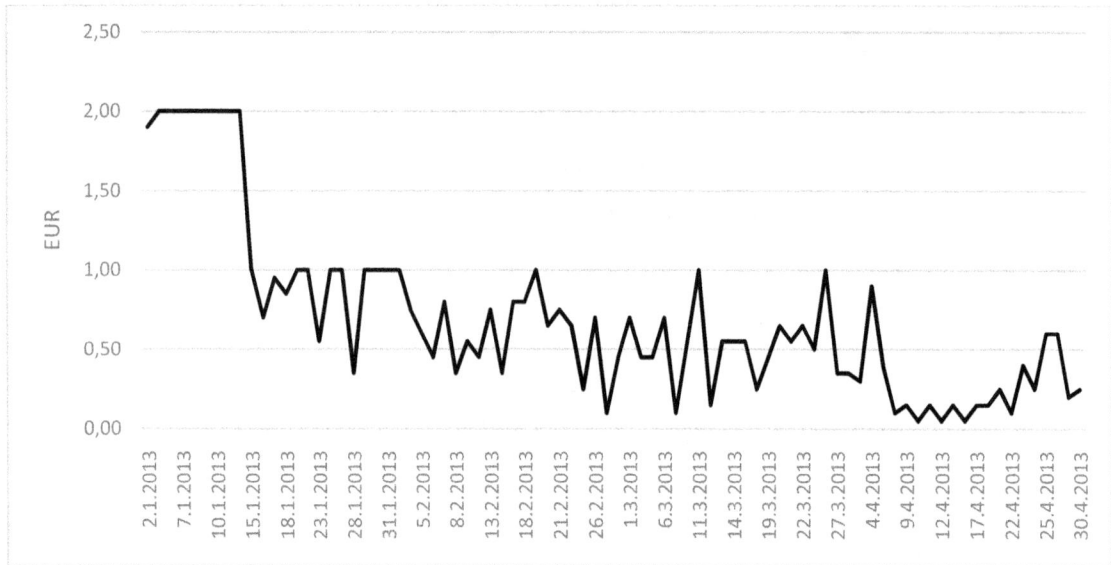

Figure 7.2. Spread in EUR for the trading time of the Stockholm monthly EPAD for May 2013 (SYSTOMAY-13)

The maximum observed spread is 2 euro and the minimum spread 0,05 euro. It is evident that the spread does not remain constant throughout the trading period.

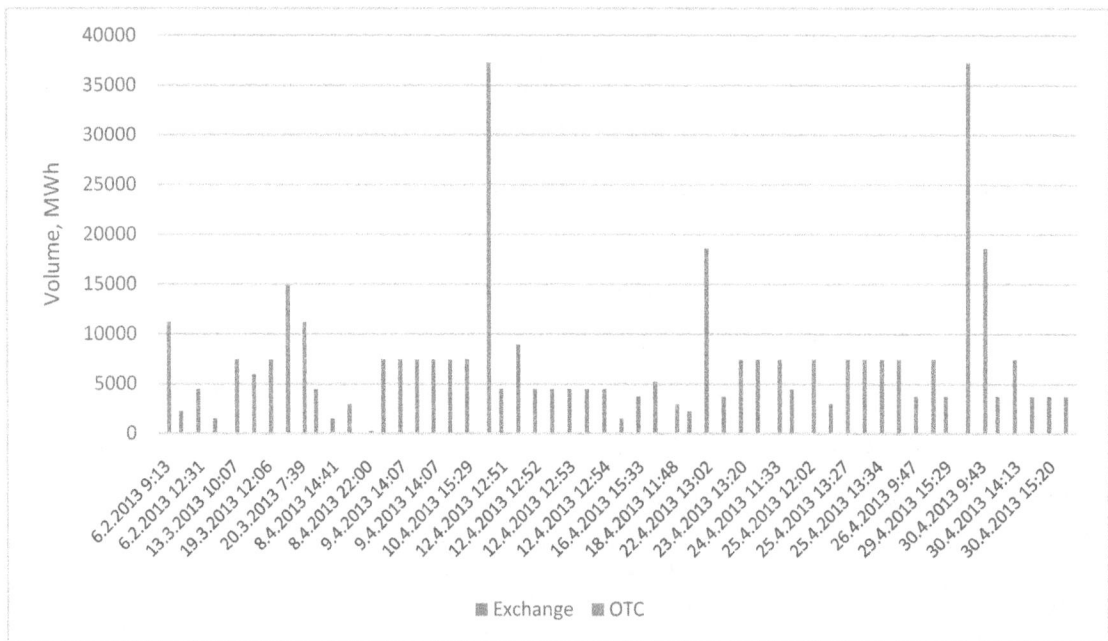

Figure 7.3. Volumes traded on the electronic trading system (ETS) and over the counter OTC during the trading period of Stockholm monthly EPAD May 2013 (SYSTOMAY-13)

Figure 7.3., shows the trading volumes of the SYSTOMAY-13 contract for the trades conducted through the electronic trading system and over the counter. The overall trading volume through the ETS is 177816 MWh and 213007 MWh OTC, the total number of trades is 54 and consists of 34 trades through the ETS and twenty OTC. The two by far largest trades have taken place OTC. Over 80% of all trades (45) took place in April, the final month of the contract trading time. There were no trades during the month of January.

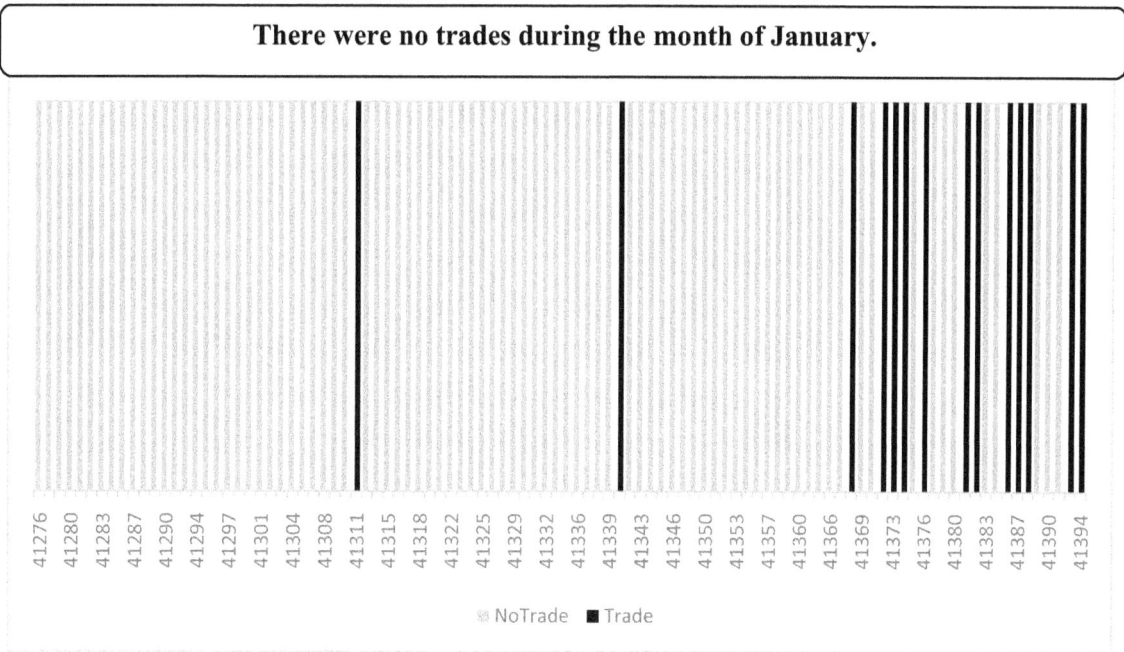

There were no trades during the month of January.

Figure 7.4. Days with and without trade on the ETS during the trading period of Stockholm monthly EPAD May 2013 (SYSTOMAY-13)

Figure 7.4. illustrates the distribution of the trading period to days with trade and to days without trade through the electronic trading system. Of the 82 trading days during the trading time of the SYSTOMAY-13 contract, there were fourteen days on which at least one trade was made through the electronic trading system. This corresponds to little over 17% of all trading days. The closing price of the SYSTOMAY-13 contract has been determined as an average of the best sell and best ask bids on 68 out of 82 trading days and on fourteen days the closing price has been determined by actual trades.

There was at least one trade through the ETS on fourteen trading days, or just over 17% of all trading days.

8. CASE 3: Helsinki Quarterly EPAD for Q2/2013 (SYHELQ2-13)

This third case turns to studying a quarterly EPAD for the second quarter of 2013 Helsinki, code SYHELQ2-13. This is a contract whose trading started on the 2nd of July 2012 and ended on the 27th March 2013. During the trading period there were 188 trading days.

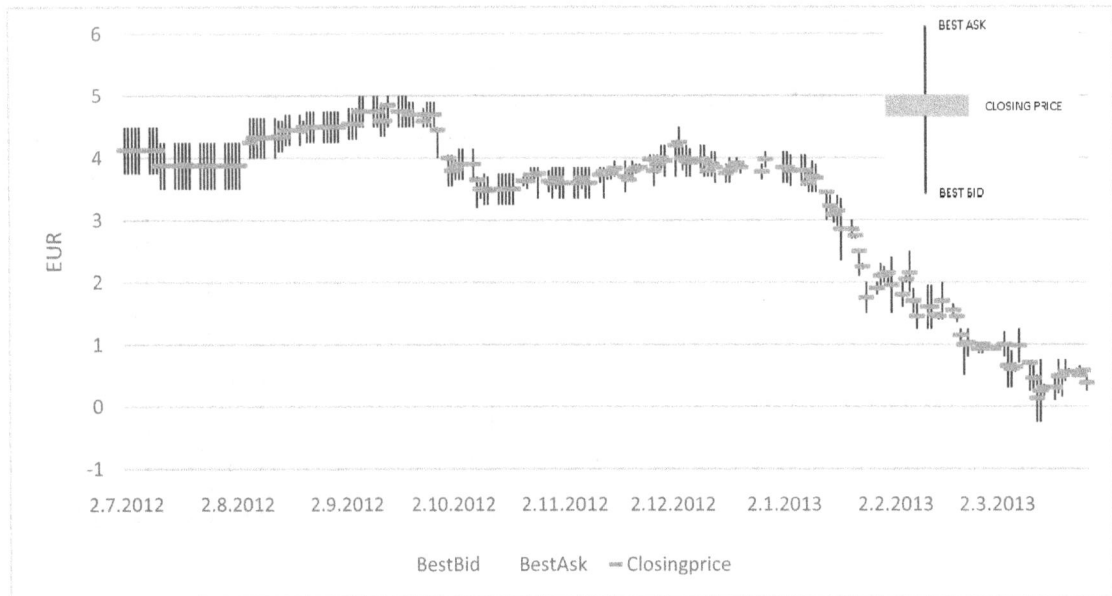

Figure 8.1. Closing price data for the trading period of Helsinki quarterly EPAD for Q2/2013 (SYSHELQ2-13), with the best bid and the best ask prices.

Figure 8.1. above shows the price development of the SYSHELQ213 EPAD contract. The difference between the daily best ask and the best bid quotes is the spread of the bids registered on the electronic trading system. For the 25 first trading days the spread is exactly 0,75 euro. The maximum observed spread is 1 euro and the minimum spread 0,05 euro. It is evident that the spread does not remain constant throughout the trading period. The average spread in EUR for the contract is 0,45 EUR. And the average spread as a percentage of the best bid price is 17,1%.

> **For the 25 first trading days the spread is exactly 0,75 euro.**

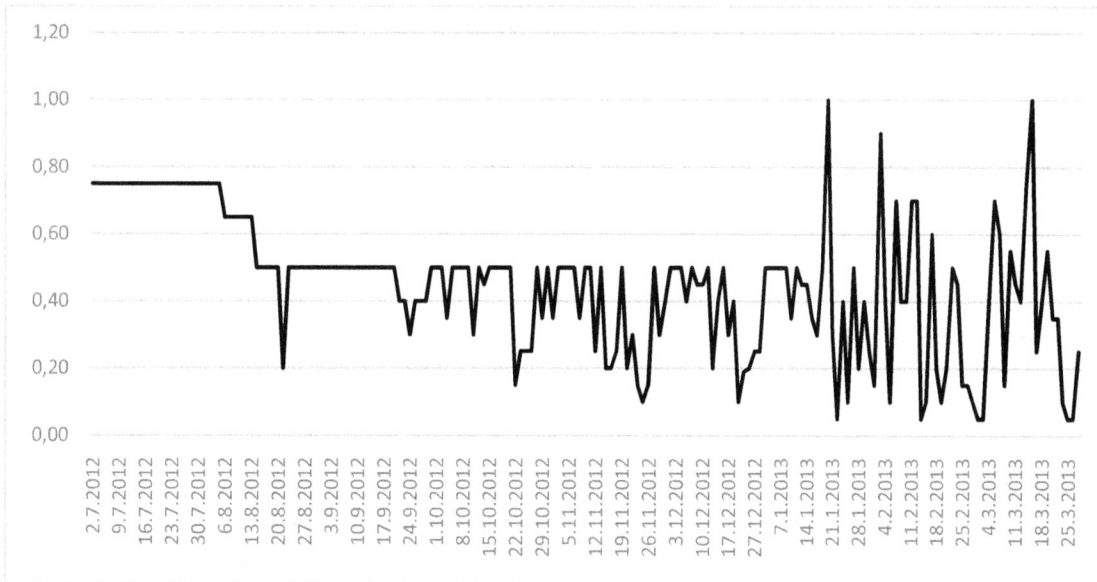

Figure 8.2. Development of the spread in EUR for the trading time of the SYHELQ2-13 quarterly contract.

Figure 8.2., shows the trading volumes of the SYHELQ2-13 contract for the trades conducted through the electronic trading system and over the counter.

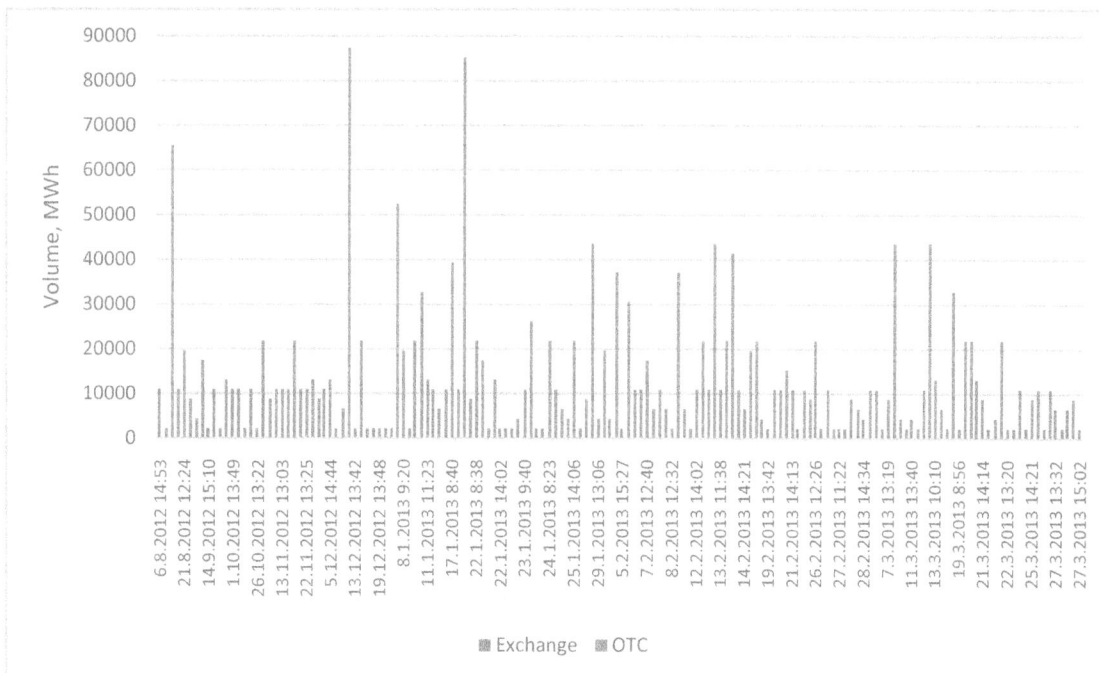

Figure 8.2. Volumes traded on the electronic trading system (ETS) and over the counter OTC during the trading period of Helsinki EPAD for the second quarter of 2013 (SYSHELQ2-13)

The overall trading volume through the ETS is 288288 MWh and 1681680 MWh OTC that is, the volume traded OTC is more than five times the size of the volume traded through the ETS. The total number of trades is 153 and consists of 42 trades through the ETS and 111 OTC. Sixteen largest trades have taken place OTC. There were no trades during the month of July.

> **The volume traded OTC is more than five times the size of the volume traded through the ETS.**

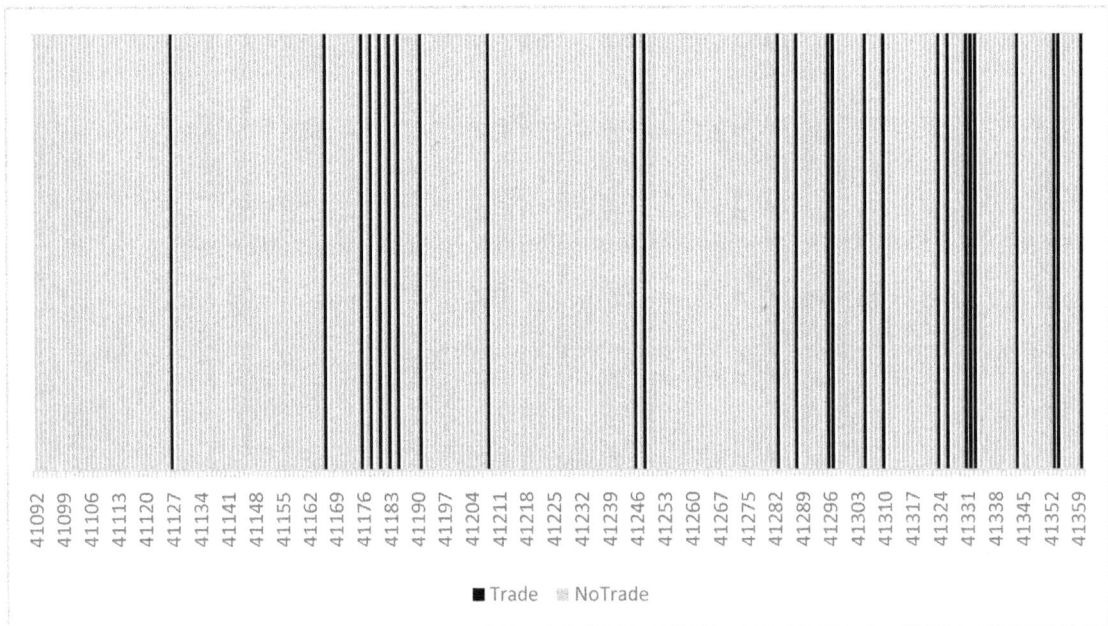

Figure 12.3. Days with and without trade on the ETS during the trading period of Helsinki EPAD for the second quarter of 2013 (SYSHELQ2-13)

Figure 8.3. illustrates the distribution of the trading period to days with trade and to days without trade through the electronic trading system. Of the 188 trading days during the trading time of the SYHELQ2-13 contract there are 26 days with at least one trade made through the electronic trading system. This corresponds to about 14% of all trading days. During the trading period, on 162 days there were no trades made through the ETS.

> **During the trading period, on 162 days there were no trades made through the ETS.**

PART IV

Preliminary Conclusions

9. Preliminary Conclusions

Here we draw some preliminary conclusions from the main findings of the report. All conclusions should be treated as preliminary and therefore only direction giving. In any case, there are many interesting issues that can be raised from the observations made in this report. In the second part of this section we propose some future research directions, based on the findings of the report.

9.1. Preliminary conclusions drawn based on the main findings

These conclusions are derived from the report and presented in no particular order.

The average daily closing price for Helsinki and Stockholm price areas differs from the average actual traded prices for contracts of all maturities for all studied years. The difference changes from year to year. This is likely to be partially due to the way the mechanism for determining the daily closing prices works.

The mechanism that is used in the determination of the daily closing price (Daily Fix) does not take into consideration the information provided by trades OTC. This means that for price areas such as Helsinki, where the great majority of the traded volume is traded OTC, a lot of to the market participants relevant information is totally omitted from the determination of the daily closing price.

On majority of trading days, during the examined period, the daily closing price is not determined based on actual trades, but by calculating the daily closing price as an average of the best bid price and the best ask price at the moment of determination of the daily closing price.

Average spreads in absolute terms (in EUR terms) seem high for monthly contracts for price areas Helsinki and Stockholm (Sweden) for all studied years – they are at an "above 0,50 EUR" level on all studied years. On absolute terms the spreads are on a lower level for quarterly and yearly contracts. Spreads are higher for the price area Helsinki than for the price area Stockholm; this may signal weaker market efficiency for Helsinki. In terms of percent (of the best ask price) the spread is over 10% for all contract maturities for Helsinki and Stockholm. An on average ten percent spread cannot be considered low.

Study of the trading time of single EPAD contracts shows that the daily spread (in absolute EUR) terms of EPAD contracts changes notably during the trading period. This signals that there is considerable uncertainty about at what price, with regards to the previous daily close a contract may be purchased or sold. Non-static spread size may signal an inefficient "weak" market.

Trading is concentrated on the OTC market as the great majority of trades, of the number of contracts traded, and of the traded volume takes place OTC. For Helsinki, during the studied years, more than 85% of the traded volume is annually traded OTC.

9.2. Future research directions

Many interesting future research directions grow from the findings and the conclusions of this report, we will list some of them using the order in which connected issues are presented in the report. Specific future research topics are listed under more general future research topics.

1. EPAD contract pricing is a topic of many interesting research possibilities:

a) What causes change in the average of the daily closing prices of EPAD contracts? Does the risk level in the markets change year to year?

b) How efficient are the EPAD markets in terms of how the closing price is determined? Comparison of the market for EPAD contracts to markets of other similar derivative contracts.

c) Is EPAD contract pricing in line with theoretical pricing of similar contracts? If not, how much and in what respect does it differ from it?

d) Do market participants consider the daily closing price (Daily Fix) as a reliable signal / benchmark about the EPAD price? How market participants price EPAD contracts in general?

e) Study of contract-by-contract average EPAD contract average prices and volatilities.

f) How market participants view the volatility on the EPAD markets in terms of how easy / difficult it is to forecast EPAD market price changes?

2. EPAD price spread is a topic that warrants more research:

a) Why do we find differences in the average absolute spreads between price areas? Why do we find differences in the average "as a % of best bid price" spreads between price areas?

b) Why do the average daily spreads for different contract maturities differ from each other? Why do the average "as a % of best bid price" spreads for different contract maturities differ from each other?

c) Why do the average daily spreads differ in different years? Why do the average "as a % of best bid price" spreads differ in different years?

d) How does the level at which EPAD contracts´ spread "exist" affect the behavior of market participants? How do market participants view the spread level?

d) How does the level of (over 10%) spread as a percentage of the best ask bid compare with the spread of other similar traded contracts, e.g., oil derivatives?

e) What does the spread level of EPAD contracts tell about the efficiency of the EPAD markets in general?

f) Why does the intra trading period spread of EPAD contracts dramatically change during the trading period?

g) How many market participants are actually bidding on the electronic trading system daily? How many market participants contribute in the creation of the spread at each time of a trading day on average?

h) How do market participants view the dramatic variability and the size of the daily spread in terms of their "market behavior"?

3. *The level of market activity in the EPAD market is a source for many interesting future research questions:*

a) How does the market on EPAD contracts compare with the markets of other comparable products markets in terms of the distribution of trades OTC / trades made through an electronic trading system?

b) Interviews of market participants about how they feel the market is functioning in terms of the distribution of where (OTC / ETS) trades are conducted. What is the reason, according to market participants, for the fact that the majority of trades are conducted OTC?

c) Why do market participants predominantly trade in yearly contracts (predominantly meaning that the majority of the overall traded volume is traded "via" yearly contracts)?

f) Why, according to market participants, the majority of the traded volume for Helsinki is traded OTC?

g) Are there "imperfections" in the ETS, according to the market participants? Is there a necessity to trade OTC due to "imperfections" in the ETS?

h) What kind of transaction cost differences are there for market participants (buyers / sellers of EPAD contracts), when trades are conducted through the ETS or OTC?

i) Are the possible transaction cost differences offset by price differences of contracts between the OTC markets and the ETS? What is the difference between the daily best ask price and the actual trades conducted on the same day OTC on average, for different years and different contract maturities?

j) Why has the volume of traded volume for Sweden decreased since the year 2010? What explains the changes in the traded volumes for different price areas?

In addition to the above listed "topical" future research directions and question there are many general future research directions. These will, however, not be listed here.

PART V

Appendix

Appendix

This appendix includes supporting materials to the report. The order in which the material is presented is in line with the presentation order of the report. The Tables in the Appendix are numbered in a way that identifies the section of the report they support, for example, Table A3.1. is the first Table that supports section 3 of the report.

Tables supporting report section 1

Table A1.1. Overview of key concepts from the financial derivatives market (Source: Nasdaq OMX)

Underlying reference prices	*Futures*: Nordic system price
	EPAD: Area price – system price
	Currency: EUR; Tick size: 0,01EUR/MWh
Contract volume and size	*Contract volume*: 1MW *Contract size*: 1MW * h in the contract
	Typical number of hours in EPAD contracts: monthly (672 - 744 h), quarterly (2159 - 2209 h), yearly (8760 - 8784 h)
Futures settlement during the trading period	*Trading day*: (Closing price - deal price) * MW * Contract hours => Daily Market Settlement
	Following day: (Closing price – previous Closing price) * MW * Contract hours => Daily Market Settlement
Futures settlement during the delivery period	*Spot reference settlement*: (avg. system price – final closing price) * Net position * hours (24) *EPAD spot reference settlement:* ((avg. area price - avg. system price) - final closing price)) * Net position * hours (24) *Expiry market settlement (DS futures, i.e. EPAD):* (final closing price - deal price) * MW * contract hours
Futures Cash Flow	
Cascading	

Tables supporting report section 3

Table A3.2. Average daily closing price in EUR for monthly, quarterly, and yearly EPAD contracts for Helsinki (HEL) and Stockholm (STO) for 2007 – 2014 (2014 data is not complete)

Delivery	MONTHLY EPAD		QUARTERLY EPAD		YEARLY EPAD	
	HEL	STO	HEL	STO	HEL	STO
2007	1,49	1,08	0,76	0,49	0,73	0,44
2008	5,81	5,56	2,57	2,19	0,89	0,46
2009	1,98	2,10	2,33	2,13	1,45	0,93
2010	1,21	1,14	1,27	1,07	1,19	0,67
2011	3,57	3,53	2,20	1,96	1,45	0,90
2012	7,32	2,92	5,00	2,98	1,91	1,44
2013	3,47	1,27	5,05	2,02	3,11	1,93
2014 (Q1)	5,53	2,41	4,71	2,48	3,70	2,23
Grand Total	3,30	2,26	2,66	1,74	1,96	1,23

Table A3.3. Average actual trade price in EUR for trades through the ETS and OTC for monthly EPAD contracts for Helsinki (HEL) and for Stockholm (STO) for years 2007 – 2014 (2014 data not complete)

Delivery	ETS		ETS Total	OTC		OTC Total	Grand Total
	HEL	STO		HEL	STO		
2007	1,6643	2,2097	1,9711	1,2220	1,4379	1,3888	1,4890
2008	6,9823	6,8037	6,8742	5,3988	6,0907	5,9689	6,1910
2009	2,7400	3,1769	3,0696	1,9967	2,3307	2,2484	2,4380
2010	1,2375	1,3097	1,2931	2,5796	2,4179	2,4650	2,0473
2011	4,8495	4,5386	4,6593	3,9947	4,4641	4,3380	4,4834
2012	7,0638	2,5752	5,3418	7,3214	3,0140	5,2509	5,2978
2013	4,4804	1,7105	3,3574	3,8349	2,0956	3,0808	3,2235
2014 (Q1)	5,8852	2,2367	4,1724	5,6817	1,8989	4,1289	4,1502
Grand Total	5,0328	2,8262	3,8123	4,2038	3,1741	3,5303	3,6438

Table A3.4. Average actual trade price in EUR for trades through the ETS and OTC for quarterly EPAD contracts for Helsinki (HEL) and Stockholm (STO) for years 2007 – 2014 (2014 data not complete)

	ETS		ETS Total	OTC		OTC Total	Grand Total
Delivery	HEL	STO		HEL	STO		
2007	1,9192	1,9880	1,9672	1,0077	0,7547	0,8302	0,8931
2008	4,7563	4,1638	4,4643	3,3152	3,2745	3,2874	3,4150
2009	2,7052	2,5771	2,6226	2,4216	2,2085	2,2779	2,3462
2010	1,4340	1,1322	1,2043	1,3752	1,3773	1,3766	1,3329
2011	2,8123	2,8304	2,8235	2,7332	3,1693	2,9807	2,9366
2012	6,2796	3,4007	4,8744	6,0586	3,6478	4,7670	4,8019
2013	4,7781	2,2181	3,7924	4,8056	2,3261	3,9624	3,9170
2014	5,7987	2,7250	4,3926	5,1382	2,8144	4,2780	4,3071
Grand Total	4,3477	2,5037	3,3067	3,6066	2,4567	2,9474	3,0304

Table A3.5. Average actual trade price in EUR for trades through the ETS and OTC for yearly EPAD contracts for Helsinki (HEL) and Stockholm (STO) for years 2007 – 2014 (2014 data not complete)

	ETS		ETS Total	OTC		OTC Total	Grand Total
Delivery	HEL	STO		HEL	STO		
2007	0,6500	0,3300	0,4367	0,5973	0,3942	0,4627	0,4625
2008	1,1836	0,4950	1,0975	1,0396	0,4951	0,7659	0,7796
2009	2,8518	1,8657	2,3308	2,2669	1,4078	1,7503	1,8101
2010	1,5490	0,9287	1,0823	1,4239	0,8038	0,9861	1,0004
2011	1,7100	1,0255	1,2794	1,7946	1,0086	1,2425	1,2483
2012	2,9963	1,8308	2,2876	2,9680	1,8028	2,2374	2,2451
2013	4,1314	2,0042	2,7331	4,3380	2,0400	3,1865	3,1159
2014	4,3877	2,2172	3,0815	4,1699	2,3651	3,3149	3,2819
Grand Total	2,9847	1,6040	2,1136	2,9403	1,4374	2,0415	2,0514

Table A3.5. Standard deviation as a percent of the average daily closing price for yearly, quarterly, and monthly EPAD contracts for Stockholm (STO) and for Helsinki (HEL) for contracts with delivery 2007 – 2014 (data for 2014 not complete)

	YEARLY EPAD		QUARTERLY EPAD		MONTHLY EPAD	
Delivery	HEL	STO	HEL	STO	HEL	STO
2007	38,8 %	47,8 %	64,1 %	101,4 %	91 %	132 %
2008	32,8 %	29,1 %	83,8 %	102,2 %	51 %	57 %
2009	60,6 %	85,8 %	49,7 %	50,4 %	63 %	58 %
2010	35,6 %	41,1 %	49,0 %	59,6 %	156 %	173 %
2011	26,8 %	43,4 %	74,4 %	85,8 %	95 %	91 %
2012	50,6 %	57,8 %	41,2 %	40,5 %	49 %	55 %
2013	58,6 %	37,1 %	38,8 %	50,2 %	67 %	100 %
2014	36,2 %	20,3 %	37,9 %	23,2 %	29 %	42 %
Grand Total	42,5 %	45,3 %	54,9 %	64,2 %	75 %	89 %

Tables supporting report section 4

Table A4.1. Average absolute (EUR) daily spreads (on the left) and the average daily spread as a percentage of the best ask price (on the right) for monthly, quarterly, and yearly contracts for Helsinki and Stockholm for the years 2007 – 2013

Delivery	HEL	STO	Grand Total	Delivery	HEL	STO	Grand Total
2007	**0,67**	**0,45**	**0,56**	**2007**	**60,3 %**	**57,5 %**	**58,9 %**
Month	0,95	0,63	0,79	Month	65,0 %	67,1 %	66,0 %
Quarter	0,52	0,31	0,42	Quarter	58,0 %	48,8 %	53,4 %
Year	0,58	0,48	0,53	Year	58,1 %	64,2 %	61,1 %
2008	**0,69**	**0,64**	**0,67**	**2008**	**25,7 %**	**32,5 %**	**29,1 %**
Month	1,19	1,12	1,15	Month	22,0 %	23,7 %	22,8 %
Quarter	0,49	0,47	0,48	Quarter	26,0 %	36,2 %	31,1 %
Year	0,33	0,26	0,29	Year	31,7 %	38,6 %	35,1 %
2009	**0,67**	**0,54**	**0,60**	**2009**	**32,8 %**	**29,8 %**	**31,3 %**
Month	1,01	0,83	0,92	Month	44,9 %	35,1 %	39,9 %
Quarter	0,64	0,52	0,58	Quarter	27,2 %	23,4 %	25,3 %
Year	0,40	0,29	0,34	Year	29,6 %	34,0 %	31,8 %
2010	**0,58**	**0,39**	**0,49**	**2010**	**55,6 %**	**47,4 %**	**51,5 %**
Month	0,98	0,59	0,78	Month	99,3 %	76,1 %	87,4 %
Quarter	0,47	0,34	0,41	Quarter	49,6 %	36,0 %	42,8 %
Year	0,44	0,31	0,38	Year	33,9 %	39,9 %	36,9 %
2011	**0,56**	**0,43**	**0,49**	**2011**	**35,0 %**	**33,8 %**	**34,4 %**
Month	0,90	0,70	0,80	Month	61,5 %	53,1 %	57,3 %
Quarter	0,50	0,42	0,46	Quarter	27,7 %	28,9 %	28,4 %
Year	0,39	0,25	0,32	Year	24,4 %	25,5 %	25,0 %
2012	**0,58**	**0,43**	**0,50**	**2012**	**15,0 %**	**18,2 %**	**16,6 %**
Month	0,99	0,75	0,87	Month	13,1 %	26,9 %	20,0 %
Quarter	0,51	0,42	0,46	Quarter	11,0 %	14,8 %	12,9 %
Year	0,37	0,21	0,29	Year	20,4 %	15,6 %	18,0 %
2013	**0,55**	**0,43**	**0,49**	**2013**	**21,1 %**	**36,4 %**	**28,6 %**
Month	0,72	0,69	0,71	Month	34,4 %	80,6 %	56,2 %
Quarter	0,51	0,38	0,44	Quarter	13,6 %	23,4 %	18,4 %
Year	0,42	0,28	0,35	Year	16,5 %	13,6 %	15,1 %
Grand Total	**0,61**	**0,47**	**0,54**	**Grand Total**	**34,2 %**	**35,8 %**	**35,0 %**

Table A4.2. Statistics for Stockholm Yearly EPAD for 2013 (SYSTOYR-13)

SYSTOYR-13	Closing Price	Deal price OTC	Deal Price ETS	Absolute Spread	Percentage Spread
Mean	1,925	2,040	2,004	0,278	13,618 %
Median	2,130	2,300	2,150	0,250	11,111 %
Mode	2,500	2,500	2,350	0,250	9,091 %
Min	0,390	0,810	0,800	0,010	1,163 %
Max	3,430	3,300	3,150	2,000	111,494 %
Skewness	-0,175	-0,586	-0,236	2,500	0,3713
Stand. dev.	0,714	0,639	0,641	0,211	10,837 %

Table A4.3. Statistics for Helsinki Monthly EPAD for March 2013 (SYHELMAR-13)

SYHELMAR13	Closing Price	Deal price OTC	Deal Price ETS	Absolute Spread	Percentage Spread
Mean	3,111	1,434	1,894	0,652	19,611 %
Median	3,550	1,350	1,350	0,725	18,182 %
Mode	4,500	0,450	1,250	1,000	20,00 %
Min	0,400	0,400	0,400	0,050	8,00 %
Max	5,000	4,750	4,650	1,000	48,718 %
Skewness	-0,295	1,367	0,762	-0,434	1,466
Stand. dev.	1,578	1,089	1,429	0,339	8,748 %

Tables supporting report section 5

Table A5.1. Cumulative EPAD trades (all contract maturities) for a given year's contracts traded through the ETS and OTC, cumulative for all price areas for years 2007 – 2013 (overall Nordic data)

Delivery	Number of trades
2007	**4197**
ETS	1611
OTC	2586
2008	**4618**
ETS	1653
OTC	2965
2009	**5748**
ETS	1941
OTC	3807
2010	**7022**
ETS	2628
OTC	4394
2011	**7900**
ETS	3227
OTC	4673
2012	**7920**
ETS	3322
OTC	4598
2013	**7231**
ETS	3061
OTC	4170
Grand Total	**44636**

Table A5.2. Number of contracts traded for each year through the ETS and OTC for years 2007 – 2013, data cumulative for all trading areas (overall Nordic data)

Delivery	Number of contracts traded
2007	**44569**
ETS	8402
OTC	36167
2008	**39213**
ETS	9140
OTC	30073
2009	**49918**
ETS	10202
OTC	39716
2010	**57957**
ETS	12869
OTC	45088
2011	**57364**
ETS	15786
OTC	41578
2012	**48518**
ETS	14074
OTC	34444
2013	**42884**
ETS	13348
OTC	29536
Grand Total	**340423**

Table A5.3. Average number of contracts per deal in Helsinki (HEL) and Stockholm (Sweden, before 2011) (STO), breakdown by contract type, contract year, and through the ETS and OTC.

Delivery	HEL	STO	Grand Total
2009	**9,38**	**11,54**	**10,83**
ETS	**4,47**	**5,87**	**5,40**
Month	6,49	7,75	7,44
Quarter	3,75	4,81	4,43
Year	3,86	4,11	3,99
OTC	**10,49**	**12,77**	**12,02**
Month	18,05	18,00	18,01
Quarter	10,45	11,95	11,46
Year	6,74	8,77	7,96
2010	**9,01**	**10,11**	**9,78**
ETS	**4,33**	**5,57**	**5,28**
Month	5,10	6,25	5,99
Quarter	3,77	5,39	5,00
Year	3,25	3,81	3,67
OTC	**10,24**	**11,90**	**11,37**
Month	13,76	17,11	16,13
Quarter	9,60	10,01	9,86
Year	7,69	8,61	8,34
2011	**7,81**	**8,83**	**8,47**
ETS	**4,93**	**5,41**	**5,22**
Month	6,18	6,40	6,31
Quarter	4,07	4,77	4,50
Year	2,84	3,82	3,46
OTC	**9,19**	**10,19**	**9,84**
Month	12,31	15,95	14,97
Quarter	9,55	9,71	9,64
Year	6,70	6,46	6,53
2012	**7,08**	**7,13**	**7,11**
ETS	**4,66**	**4,54**	**4,60**
Month	5,90	6,27	6,04
Quarter	3,57	3,70	3,63
Year	2,71	3,22	3,02
OTC	**8,43**	**8,07**	**8,23**
Month	12,92	15,00	13,92
Quarter	8,44	8,93	8,70
Year	5,97	5,49	5,67
2013	**5,83**	**7,13**	**6,40**
ETS	**4,18**	**4,50**	**4,32**
Month	5,01	6,00	5,42

Quarter	3,38	3,51	3,43
Year	2,22	2,75	2,57
OTC	**6,53**	**8,32**	**7,30**
Month	9,25	13,98	11,30
Quarter	7,58	10,44	8,55
Year	4,03	4,91	4,47
Q1 2014	**5,69**	**6,66**	**6,13**
ETS	**4,06**	**4,88**	**4,47**
Month	5,79	7,52	6,60
Quarter	3,15	4,10	3,58
Year	2,24	2,69	2,51
OTC	**6,15**	**7,33**	**6,66**
Month	12,48	15,63	13,77
Quarter	7,18	7,76	7,39
Year	3,82	5,45	4,60
Grand Total	**7,20**	**8,85**	**8,16**

Table A5.3. Cont. Average number of contracts per deal in Helsinki (HEL) and Stockholm (Sweden, before 2011) (STO), breakdown by contract type, contract year, and through the ETS and OTC.

Table A5.4. Volume turnover (TWh) for years 2007 – 2013, cumulative for all price areas including volume traded OTC and through the ETS for all contract maturities. All Swedish price areas cumulated in to SWE

Delivery	SWE	HEL	ARH	CPH	GER	OSL	TAL	TRO	Grand Total
2007	36,1735	19,0488	24,2786	10,4816	33,4112	7,5743			130,9680
2008	40,1834	21,1026	16,5548	3,4649	36,8670	5,5140			123,6867
2009	77,8211	36,5782	19,6419	5,2989	2,4703	4,4141			146,2247
2010	102,0555	39,2590	20,3879	6,2457		3,9297			171,8777
2011	89,0535	43,2501	21,5688	7,9654		4,2338		0,0190	166,0907
2012	84,2931	47,9420	17,1387	5,1865		2,5464		0,4342	157,5409
2013	58,9952	42,1094	12,6490	7,4523		2,1348	0,0925	0,5499	123,9830
Grand Total	488,5753	249,2900	132,2197	46,0953	72,7485	30,3472	0,0925	1,0031	1020,3717

Table A5.5. Overall volume traded (GWh) and the distribution of traded volume between the trades conducted through the ETS and OTC (in percent) 2007 – 2013 including all contract types

Delivery	ETS	ETS % of Total	OTC	OTC % Total	Grand Total
2007	27690,11	21,14 %	103277,90	78,86 %	130968,01
2008	19994,45	16,17 %	103692,29	83,83 %	123686,74
2009	22902,61	15,66 %	123322,06	84,34 %	146224,66
2010	28816,89	16,77 %	143060,83	83,23 %	171877,72
2011	33797,94	20,35 %	132292,73	79,65 %	166090,67
2012	30584,00	19,41 %	126956,88	80,59 %	157540,88
2013	26634,63	21,48 %	97348,38	78,52 %	123983,01
Grand Total	190420,62	18,66 %	829951,07	81,34 %	1020371,69

Table A5.6. Total volume traded (GWh) through the ETS and OTC for Helsinki. (2006 and 2014 not full data)

Delivery	ETS	OTC	Grand Total
2006	405,49	6767,405	7172,895
2007	321,139	18727,63	19048,77
2008	1312,599	19789,98	21102,58
2009	2879,201	33699,05	36578,25
2010	2837,241	36421,71	39258,95
2011	5421,911	37828,17	43250,08
2012	6266,265	41675,69	47941,96
2013	4836,166	37273,2	42109,37
Q1 2014	3376,402	32978,68	36355,08
Grand Total	27656,414	265161,5	292817,9

Table 6 Total volume traded (GWh) through the ETS and OTC for Sweden. (2006and 2014 not full data)

Delivery	ETS	OTC	Grand Total
2006	89,569	8112,485	8202,054
2007	521,333	35652,1466	36173,4796
2008	1303,295	38880,1431	40183,4381
2009	5127,14	72693,9904	77821,1304
2010	11209,192	90846,2908	102055,4828
2011	11177,346	77876,196	89053,542
2012	12263,358	72029,722	84293,08
2013	10893,122	48102,0406	58995,1626
Q1 2014	8307,203	44818,1515	53125,3545
Grand Total	60891,558	489011,166	549902,724

Table A5.8. Total volume traded (GWh) through the ETS and OTC for Århus. (2006 and 2014 not full data)

Delivery	ETS	OTC	Grand Total
2006	13476,722	3377,882	16854,6
2007	17015,84	7262,784	24278,62
2008	9931,025	6623,748	16554,77
2009	11409,3	8232,626	19641,93
2010	11069,76	9318,103	20387,86
2011	11884,918	9683,899	21568,82
2012	8652,984	8485,762	17138,75
2013	6739,135	5909,822	12648,96
Q1 2014	4226,691	5204,146	9430,837
Grand Total	**94406,375**	**64098,77**	**158505,1**

Tables supporting reported Case 1

Table A6.1. Statistics collected for the Helsinki Monthly EPAD for May 2013 (SYHELMAY-13)

SYHELMAY-13	Closing Price	Deal Price ETS	Deal Price OTC	Absolute Spread	Percentage Spread
Mean	1,397	0,729	0,639	0,861	77,90 %
Median	0,750	0,550	0,275	0,925	51,67 %
Mode	4,000	0,550	0,200	1,000	40,00 %
Min	-0,080	0,200	0,050	0,100	7,41 %
Max	4,000	2,400	3,350	2,000	350,00 %
Skewness	0,856	2,147	2,506	1,030	1,89
Stand. Dev.	1,354	0,601	0,899	0,488	60,73 %

Table A6.2. Overview of market activity for Helsinki Monthly EPAD May 2013 (SYHELMAY-13)

SYHELMAY-13	ETS	OTC	Grand Total
Sum of the Number of Contracts Traded	57,00	83,40	140,40
Average Contracts per Deal	4,07	5,96	5,01
Sum of Volume Traded (MWh)	42408,00	62049,60	104457,60
Average Volume per Deal (MWh)	3029,14	4432,11	3730,63

Tables supporting reported Case 2

Table A7.1. Statistics collected for the Stockholm Monthly EPAD for May 2013 (SYSTOMAY-13)

SYSTOMAY-13	Closing Price	Deal price OTC	Deal Price Exchange	Absolute Spread	Percentage Spread
Mean	0,467	0,109	0,092	0,698	105,77 %
Median	0,400	0,050	0,000	0,575	91,67 %
Mode	1,000	0,000	0,000	1,000	100,00 %
Min	-0,300	-0,050	-0,050	0,050	5,00 %
Max	1,180	0,800	0,800	2,000	500,00 %
Skewness	0,316	2,465	2,604	1,296	316,38 %
Stand. Dev.	0,387	0,228	0,212	0,539	82,67 %

Table A7.2. Overview of market activity for Stockholm Monthly EPAD May 2013 (SYSTOMAY-13)

SYSTOMAY-13	ETS	OTC	Grand Total
Sum of the Number of Contracts Traded	209,0	211,3	420,3
Average Contracts per Deal	6,5	11,7	8,4
Sum of Volume Traded (MWh)	155496,0	157207,2	312703,2
Average Volume per Deal (MWh)	4859,3	8733,7	6254,1

Tables supporting reported Case 3

Table A8.1. Statistics collected for Helsinki Quarterly EPAD for the second quarter of 2013 (SYHELQ2-13)

SYHELQ2-13	Closing Price	Deal price OTC	Deal Price Exchange	Absolute Spread	Percentage Spread
Mean	3,299	2,542	2,231	0,454	17,08 %
Median	3,800	2,725	1,900	0,500	12,14 %
Mode	3,880	4,000	1,500	0,500	17,65 %
Min	0,130	0,500	0,300	0,050	1,82 %
Max	4,850	4,850	4,650	1,000	150,00 %
Skewness	-1,114	-0,065	0,248	-0,021	407,04 %
Stand. Dev.	1,306	1,510	1,356	0,203	19,04 %

Table A8.2. Overview of market activity for Helsinki Quarterly EPAD for the second quarter of 2013 (SYHELQ2-13)

SYHELQ2-13	ETS	OTC	Grand Total
Sum of the Number of Contracts Traded	132,00	770,00	902,00
Average Contracts per Deal	3,00	6,36	5,47
Sum of Volume Traded (MWh)	288288,00	1681680,00	1969968,00
Average Volume per Deal (MWh)	6552,00	13898,18	11939,20

www.ingramcontent.com/pod-product-compliance
Lightning Source LLC
Chambersburg PA
CBHW051118200326
41518CB00016B/2550